SING TOGETHER!

SING TOGETHER!

ONE HUNDRED SONGS FOR UNISON SINGING

Arranged by
WILLIAM APPLEBY and FREDERICK FOWLER

OXFORD UNIVERSITY PRESS
MUSIC DEPARTMENT GREAT CLARENDON STREET OXFORD OX2 6DP

ALPHABETICAL LIST OF CONTENTS—*SEE OVERLEAF*

ALPHABETICAL LIST OF CONTENTS

(First lines in italics)

ALPHABETICAL LIST OF CONTENTS

ACKNOWLEDGMENTS

Thanks are due as follows for permission to reprint words and melodies:

Allans Music (Australia) Pty. Ltd.—(*words and melody*): Waltzing Matilda.

American Folklore Society Inc.—(*words and melody*): Scraping up Sand.

E. J. Arnold & Son Ltd.—(*words and melody*): Green and White.

C. C. Birchard & Co.—(*words*): The Cobbler and the Crow.

Boosey & Hawkes Ltd.—(*words*): The Flight of the Earls (from the *New National Song Book*).

Co-operative Recreation Service Inc.—(*words and melody*): The Cuckoo.

J. Curwen & Sons Ltd.—(*words and melodies*): This Old Man, Boney was a Warrior, Blow away the Morning Dew, The Wraggle Taggle Gipsies.

E. P. Dutton & Co. Inc.—(*words and melody*): Sacramento (collected by Stan Hugill).

Mrs. MacMahon and University of London Press—(*words and melody*): The Fox's Song.

Thomas Nelson & Sons Ltd.—(*words*): What shall we do with the Drunken Sailor? (2 verses), The Mallow Fling.

Novello & Co. Ltd.—(*words*): The Gay Musician, (*melody*): Elsie Marley, (*words and melodies*): There was a Jolly Miller, The Keeper, The Farmyard, John Barleycorn, The Tree in the Wood (collected by Cecil Sharp), High Germany (collected by H. E. D. Hammond).

Oxford University Press—(*words*): The Riddle, Andulko, Ho-la-hi, Captain Morgan's March (from Oxford School Music Books); The Smuggler's Song (from Clarendon Class Singing Course); Fisherman's Night Song; Spring Song (from Sixty Songs for Little Children); Punchinello, The Merry Cobbler (from A Second Sixty Songs); Anna Marie, Come Home Now (from A Third Sixty Songs); The Shepherdess (from the Clarendon Song Books); (*words and melodies*): Donkey Riding, Rio Grande, What shall we do with the Drunken Sailor? (from the Oxford Song Books).

The Peacock Collection, National Museum of Canada—(*words and melody*): I'se the B'y.

Routledge & Kegan Paul Ltd.—(*words and melody*): Sacramento (collected by Stan Hugill).

Frederick Ungar Publishing Co.—(*words and melody*): Jim along Josie (from The American Play-Party Song by B. A. Botkin, © 1937, 1963 by B. A. Botkin).

A Melody Edition is on sale.

1. THE NOBLE DUKE OF YORK

English traditional song

Boldly
VOICE
PIANO
mf
Oh, the no-ble Duke of York, He had ten thou-sand
cresc.
men, He marched them up to the top of the hill And he marched them down a-gain.
dim.
FINE
mp
1. And when they were up they were up, And when they were down they were down, And when they were on-ly half way up They were neith-er up nor down.
2. They look'd all a-round and a-round, But noth-ing at all could they find, Ex-cept a big hay-stack in a field, And that they left be-hind.
3. The Eng-lish-man said, "Tis a stack," The Scots-man he said, "Nay," The I-rish-man said it was a church With the stee-ple blown a-way.
Oh, the
R.H.
D.S.

Printed in Great Britain
OXFORD UNIVERSITY PRESS, MUSIC DEPARTMENT, GREAT CLARENDON STREET, OXFORD OX2 6DP

2. MY FATHER'S GARDEN

French traditional song, with words by Frederick Fowler

Simply
VOICE
PIANO
mp
1.&2. My fa - ther has a gar - den With
ma - ny li - lac trees, My fa - ther has a gar - den With
ma - ny li - lac trees,
(1.)With branch-es spread -ing sky - wards And
(2.)With branch-es for the birds' nests And
sway - ing in the breeze.
flow - ers for the bees.
Come in-to our gar - den, come and see the
li - lacs there, Come in-to our gar - den, li - lacs ev - 'ry - where!
D.S.

3. MY AUNT JEMIMA

Traditional German tune

Steadily
VOICE
PIANO
mp
mp
Now I'm going to sing to you 'Bout my Aunt Je - mi - ma. She made plas - ter of the best Down in Ca - ro - li - na.
Sheep-skin and the bees' good wax, Thun-der-pitch for plas - ter: If you try to pull it off, It will stick the fas - ter.
Skin a ma, lick ma, doo - dle di, Skin a ma, lick ma di - do. Skin a ma, lick ma, doo-dle di, Skin a ma, lick ma di - do.

4. SKIP TO MY LOU

American folk-song

Simply
VOICE
PIANO
mp
Lou, Lou, skip to my Lou; Lou, Lou,
skip to my Lou; Lou, Lou, skip to my Lou; Skip to my Lou, my dar - ling.
FINE
p
1. Lost my part - ner, what'll I do? Lost my part - ner, what'll I do?
2. I'll find a-nother one pretty as you, I'll find a-nother one pretty as you,
Lost my part - ner, what'll I do? Skip to my Lou, my dar - ling.
I'll find a-nother one pretty as you, Skip to my Lou, my dar - ling.
D.S.

3 Cows in the meadow, Moo, Moo, Moo!

4 Flies in the sugar bowl, Shoo, Shoo, Shoo!

5. JIM ALONG JOSIE

American folk-song

Lightly

VOICE

mp

1. Hey, jim a - long, jim a-long Jo - sie, Hey, jim a - long, jim a-long Jo. Hey, jim a - long, jim a-long Jo - sie, Hey, jim a - long, jim a-long Jo.
2. Walk jim a - long, jim a-long Jo - sie, Walk jim a - long, jim a-long Jo. Walk jim a - long, jim a-long Jo - sie, Walk jim a - long, jim a-long Jo.

PIANO

mp

D.S.

3 Hop jim along
4 Run jim along
5 Jump jim along
6 Crawl jim along
7 Swing jim along
8 Roll jim along

Jim along = jog along

6. SPRING SONG

German folk-song; English version by Frances B. Wood

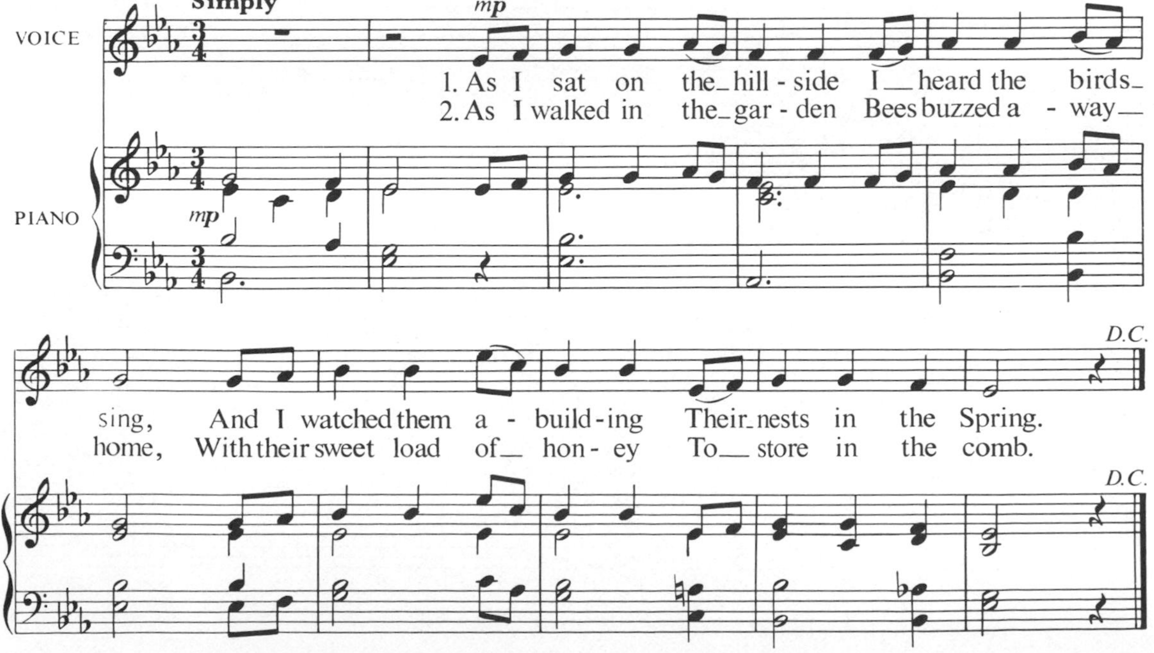
Simply
VOICE
mp
1. As I sat on the hill - side I heard the birds sing, And I watched them a - build - ing Their nests in the Spring.
2. As I walked in the gar - den Bees buzzed a - way home, With their sweet load of hon - ey To store in the comb.
PIANO
mp
D.C.

7. PUNCHINELLO

French folk-song; English version by Frances B. Wood

Lively
mf
VOICE
PIANO
mf
1."Look, who comes here! Why it's Mis - ter Punch - i - nel - lo. Look! Punch and Ju - dy are back a-gain to town. Where have you been?— We've missed you, Punch-i - nel - lo." "Here, there, and else - where, Wand - 'ring up and down."
2."Play for us now; we are read - y, Punch - i - nel - lo. Play for us now; we all love to watch your fun." Round comes the hat — and in we pop our pen - nies. "Thank you," says Ju - dy, "Thank you, ev - 'ry one."
D.C.
D.C.

The words have been slightly adapted.

8. THE MERRY COBBLER

Belgian folk-song; English version by Frances B. Wood

Simply
VOICE
PIANO
mp
mp
1. I cob - ble, cob - ble all day long
2. With tap, tap, tap, I heel and sole;
Tra, la - de - dee - ra.
And, as I work, I sing this song.
With stitch, stitch, stitch, I make shoes whole.
Tra, la - de - fal - de - dee, Tra, la - de - dee - ra.
D.C.
D.C.

3 Just send your boots and shoes to me,
No matter how worn out they be.

4 Then back they'll come as good as new.
Yes, I'm the cobbler man for you.

The words have been slightly adapted.

9. THE RIDDLE

German folk-song, translated by Elizabeth Fiske

Moderato
VOICE
PIANO
p
1. A lit - tle man is standing with - in the wood; He wears a pur - ple cloak and a small black hood. Tell me, tell me if you can, What's the name of this small man, In a pur - ple cloak_ and a small black hood?
2. The lit - tle man is si - lent and makes no sound; He stands with on - ly one foot up - on the ground. Tell me who this man can be, For he will not an - swer me, Stand-ing there with one_ foot up - on the ground.
mp
D.C.

10. GREEN AND WHITE

German folk-song, translated by John Horton

Simply
VOICE
PIANO
mp
mp
1. Green, green, green's the co-lour of my gar-ments, Green, green, green my on-ly wear shall be. If you'd have me tell you why I love it dear-ly: My true love a game-keep-er is he!
2. White, white, white's the co-lour of my gar-ments, White, white, white my on-ly wear shall be. If you'd have me tell you why I love it dear-ly: My true love a ba-ker's man is he!
D.C.
D.C.

11. JOHN SMITH, FELLOW FINE

Scottish folk-song

Clearly
VOICE
PIANO
mp
mp
1. John Smith, fel-low fine, Can you shoe this horse o' mine? Yes, Sir, that I can, Just as well as a-ny man.
3. Scam-per, scam-per well, Make the po-ny scam-per well, Scam-per, scam-per well, Make the po-ny scam-per well.
FINE
FINE
mf
mf
2. There's a nail up-on the toe: The po-ny then will want to go.
There's a nail up-on the heel To make the po-ny scam-per well.
D. S. al Fine
D. S. al Fine

12. COME HOME NOW

Westphalian traditional tune, with English words by Helen Henschel

VOICE
PIANO
Con ped.
Come home now, come
home now, The bask-et's full, the work is done; Come home now, come
home now, Our work to-day is done.—— We've earned our sup - per,
you'll a-gree, And we're as hung - ry as can be; Come
home now, come home now, Our work to-day is done.

13. THE GAY MUSICIAN

German folk-song; English version by Laurence Swinyard

Che rfully
VOICE
PIANO
mp
Verses 1. 2&3. I am a gay mu-si - cian, I come from far a-
-way, I am a gay mu - si - cian, I come from far a - way.
*A
f
I play so
B
p
gai - ly, (He plays so
A
f
gai - ly,)
(1.)Up-on my trum - pet, (Up-on his
(2.)Up-on my picco - lo, (Up-on his
(3.)Up-on my big drum, (Up-on his
B
p
A+B
mf
trum - pet,) Ta - ran - ta-ra, ta - ran - ta-ra, ta - ran - ta-ra - ta - ray.
picco - lo,) (whistle -)
big drum,) Pom-pom - ti-pom,pom-pom - ti-pom,pom-pom - ti-pom-pom-pay.
D.C.
D.C.

* One group may sing the phrases marked A, another those marked B.

14. THE FOX'S SONG

Brightly
VOICE
PIANO
mp
1. A sly old fox am I, And in the farm near by, I hear the geese say "Clack, clack, clack," The ducks say "Quack, quack, quack." A sly old fox am I.
2. At night when they're a-sleep In-to the yard I creep; A goose up-on my back I throw, Then quick-ly home I go. A sly old fox am I.
3. The far-mer he has come To shoot me with his gun, But though he search-es ev-'ry-where, He can-not find my lair. A sly old fox am I.
1. 2.
D.S.
Last time

15. ANNA MARIE

Dutch tune; words by E.L.

Lightly
VOICE
PIANO
mp
1. Oh, where are you go-ing, my An-na Ma-rie? Oh, where are you go-ing, my An-na Ma-rie? Going to Lon-don the sol-diers to see,
2. Oh, what are you seek-ing, my An-na Ma-rie? Oh, what are you seek-ing, my An-na Ma-rie? Seek-ing a hus-band wher-ev-er he be,
3. Oh, what are you look-ing for, An-na Ma-rie? Oh, what are you look-ing for, An-na Ma-rie? Look-ing for Mo-ther to get me my tea,
Hop sa sa, fa la la, An-na Ma-rie.
mf
f
Going to Lon-don the sol-diers to see,
Seek-ing a hus-band wher-ev-er he be,
Look-ing for Mo-ther to get me my tea,
Hop sa sa, fa la la, An-na Ma-rie.
D.C.
Smiling
Indignant
Toss of Head

16. MICHAEL FINNIGIN

English traditional song

Merrily
VOICE
PIANO
mp
1. There was an old man called Michael Finnigin, He grew whiskers on his chin-i-gin, The wind came up and blew them in-i-gin, Poor old Michael Fin-ni-gin. (Be-gin-i-gin.) 2. There
was an old man called Michael Finnigin, He kicked up an aw-ful din-i-gin, Be-cause they said he must not sing-i-gin, Poor old Michael Fin-ni-gin. (Be-gin-i-gin.) 3. There
FINE
D.S.

3 There was an old man called Michael Finnigin,
He went fishing with a pinigin,
Caught a fish but dropped it inigin,
Poor *etc.*

4 There was an old man called Michael Finnigin,
Climbed a tree and barked his shinigin,
Took off several yards of skinigin,
Poor *etc.*

5 There was an old man called Michael Finnigin,
He grew fat and then grew thinigin,
Then he died, and had to beginigin,
Poor old Michael Finnigin *STOP!* (*shouted*).

17. THIS OLD MAN

English traditional song

Moderato
VOICE
PIANO
mp
This old man he played {one, two,
He played nick-nack
on my {drum. shoe.
mf
Nick-nack pad-dy-whack, give a dog a bone; This old man came roll-ing home.
D.S.

3 – knee 4 – door 5 – hive 6 – sticks 7 – up in heaven 8 – gate 9 – line 10 – hen

18. THE KEEPER

English folk-song

Steadily
VOICE
PIANO
mp
1. The keep - er did a - shoot - ing go, And un - der his cloak he carried a bow,
2. The first doe he shot at he missed, The sec - ond doe he trimmed he kissed, The
3. The fourth doe she did cross the plain, The keep - er fetched her back a - gain,

All for to shoot at a mer-ry lit-tle doe
third doe went where no - bo-dy wist
Where she is now she may re - main
A - mong the leaves so
green O.
mf
*A
B
A
B
Jack-ie Boy! Mas - ter! Sing ye well! Ve - ry well!
8ve
A
B
A
A+B
Hey down, Ho down, der-ry der-ry down, A-mong the leaves so
green O.
mp
A
B
To my hey down down, To my ho down down,
A
B
A
A+B
mf
D.C.
Hey down, Ho down, der-ry der-ry down, A-mong the leaves so green O.

*One group may sing the phrases marked A, another those marked B.

19. TEN IN THE BED

English traditional song

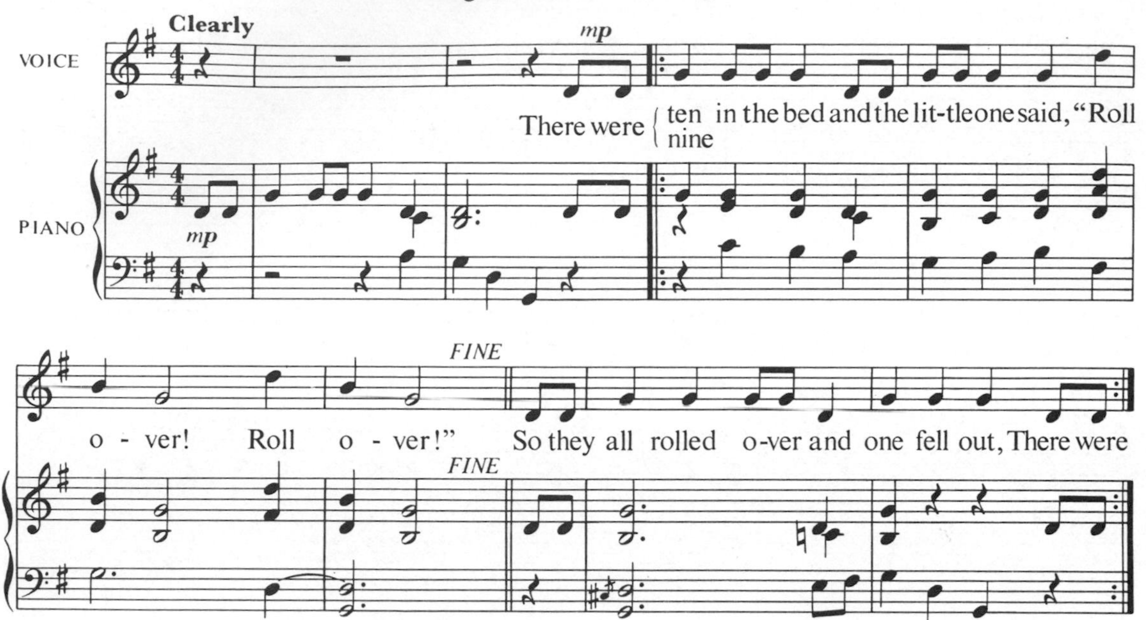
Clearly
VOICE
PIANO
mp
There were { ten / nine } in the bed and the lit-tle one said, "Roll
o - ver! Roll o - ver!"
FINE
So they all rolled o-ver and one fell out, There were

v. 2 nine, v. 3 eight etc., until the last time:
There were none in the bed, so no one said, "Roll over! Roll over!"

20. ONE MAN WENT TO MOW

English traditional song

Clearly
VOICE
PIANO
mp
One man went to mow, Went to mow a mea-dow,
One man and his dog Went to mow a mea-dow.
Two men went to mow,
Three men etc.

Went to mow a mea-dow,— Two men, one man, and his dog Went to mow a mea-dow.—
*

* Repeat this chord, as required, for numbers larger than two.

21. THERE WAS A JOLLY MILLER

English folk-song

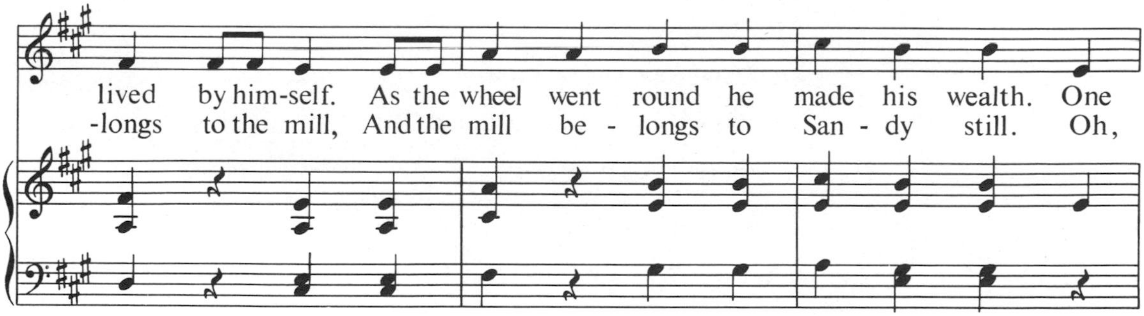

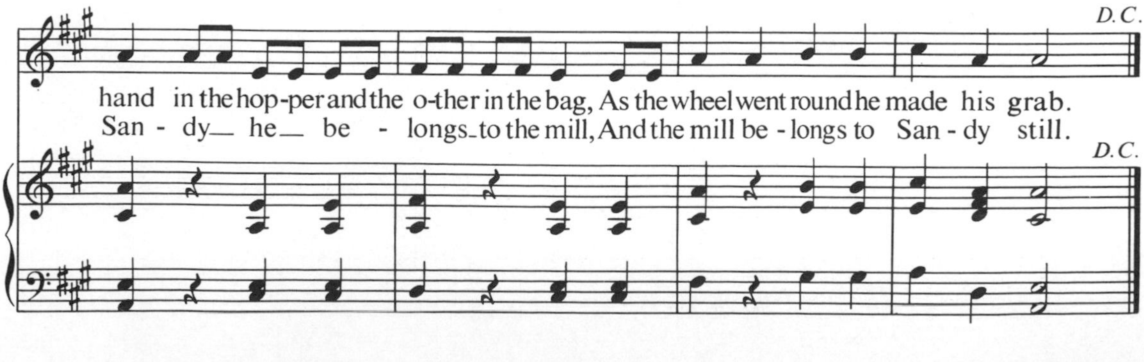

Briskly

VOICE

PIANO

mf

1. There was a jol-ly mil-ler and he lived by him-self. As the wheel went round he made his wealth. One hand in the hop-per and the o-ther in the bag, As the wheel went round he made his grab.

2. Oh, San - dy— he— be - longs to the mill, And the mill be - longs to San - dy still. Oh, San - dy— he— be - longs—to the mill, And the mill be - longs to San - dy still.

D.C.

22. BONEY WAS A WARRIOR

English sea shanty. 'Boney' is Napoleon Bonaparte.

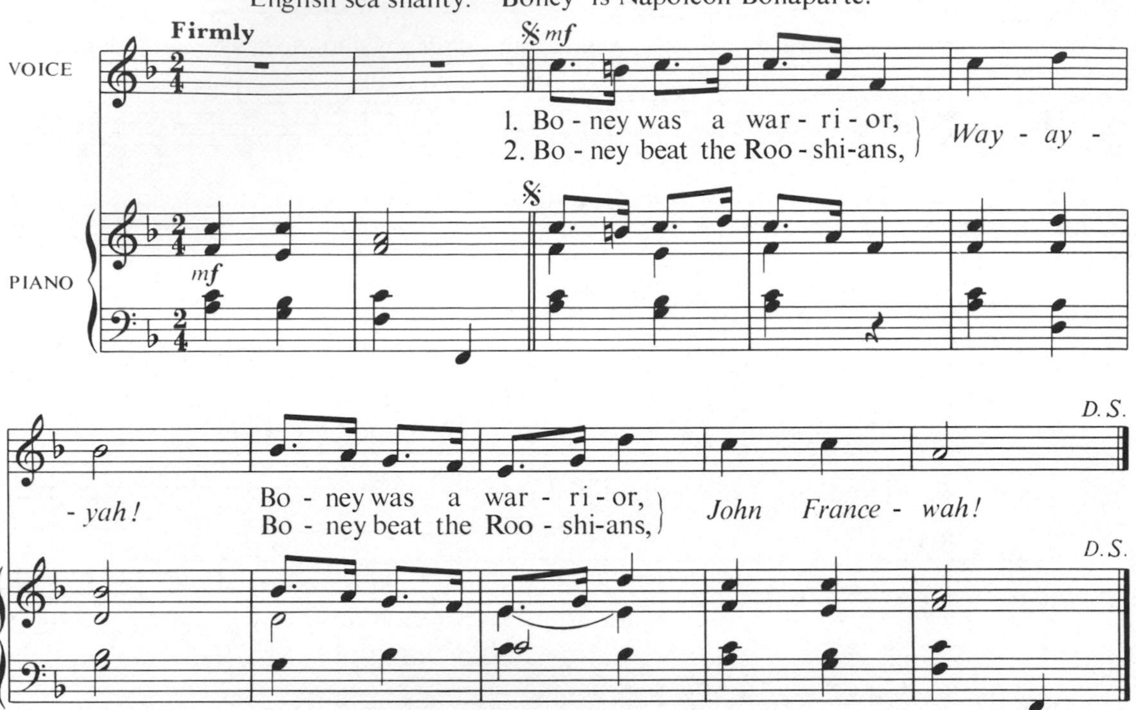
Firmly
VOICE
PIANO
mf
1. Bo - ney was a war - ri - or,
2. Bo - ney beat the Roo - shi-ans,
Way - ay -
- yah!
Bo - ney was a war - ri - or,
Bo - ney beat the Roo - shi-ans,
John France - wah!
D.S.

3 Boney beat the Prooshians,

4 Boney went to Mossycow,

5 Boney he came back again,

6 Boney went to El-be-ah,

7 Boney went to Waterloo,

8 Boney he was sent away,

9 Boney broke his heart and died,

10 Boney was a warrior.

23. DOWN IN DEMERARA

British student song

Briskly
VOICE
PIANO
mp
1. There was a man who
2. Now that poor horse he

had a hors-e-lum, had a hors-e-lum, had a hors-e-lum, Was a man who
fell a sick-e-lum, fell a sick-e-lum, fell a sick-e-lum, That poor horse he
had a hors-e-lum, Down in De - me - ra - ra.
fell a sick-e-lum, Down in De - me - ra - ra.
mf
And here we sit like
mf
birds in the wil-der-ness, birds in the wil-der-ness, birds in the wil-der-ness,
D. S.
Here we sit like birds in the wil-der-ness, Down in De - me - ra - ra.
D. S.

3 Now that poor man he sent for a doctorum.

4 Now that poor horse he went and diedalum.

5 And here we sit and flap our wingsalum.

24. DONKEY RIDING

English traditional sea song

Briskly
VOICE
PIANO
mf
1. Were you e - ver in Que - bec,
2. Were you e - ver off Cape Horn,
3. Were you ever in Car - diff Bay,
Stow- ing tim - ber on the deck,
Where it's al - ways fine and warm,
Where the folks all shout, "Hur - ray!
Where there's a king with a gol - den crown,
And seen the lion and the un - i - corn,
Here comes John with his three months' pay
Rid - ing on a don - key?
Rid - ing on a don - key?
Rid - ing on a don - key?"
f
Hey! ho! a - way we go,
p
Don - key rid - ing,
don - key rid - ing,
Hey! ho! a - way we go,
Rid - ing on a don - key.
D.C.

25. WHAT SHALL WE DO WITH THE DRUNKEN SAILOR?

English sea shanty

Not too fast
VOICE
PIANO
mf
1. What shall we do with the drunk- en sail - or,
2. Put him in the long-boat un - til he's so - ber,
What shall we do with the drunk-en sail - or, What shall we do with the drunk-en sail - or
Put him in the long-boat un - til he's so - ber, Put him in the long-boat un - til he's so - ber
mp
*Ear - ly in the morn - ing?
Ear - ly in the morn - ing.
Hoo - ray and up she ris - es, Hoo - ray and
up she ris - es, Hoo - ray and up she ris - es *Ear - ly in the morn - ing.
D.C.

*pronounced 'Er-lye'

3 Pull out the plug and wet him all over.

4 Put him in the scuppers with a hose-pipe on him.

26. FIRE DOWN BELOW

English sea shanty

Firmly
VOICE
PIANO
mf
L.H.
1. Fire in the gal - ley, fire down be - low,
2. Fire in the fore - peak, fire down be - low,
It's
fetch a buck-et o' wa - ter, boys, there's fire down be - low.
f
Fire! fire!
fire down be - low, It's fetch a buck-et o' wa - ter, boys, there's fire down be- low.
D. S.
D. S.

3 Fire up aloft and fire down below,
It's fetch a bucket of water, boys, there's fire down below.
Fire! fire! etc.

4 Fire in the galley, fire down below,
It's fire in the cabin, but the captain doesn't know.
Fire! fire! etc.

27. THE FARMYARD

English folk-song

Moderato
mp
VOICE
PIANO
mp
1. & 2. Up was I on my fa-ther's farm On a May day morn-ing
ear - ly, (1.) Feed-ing of my fa-ther's cows (2.) Feed-ing of my fa-ther's goats On a May day morn-ing ear - ly. (1.) With a (2.) With a
moo, moo here, and a moo, moo there, Here a moo, there a moo, here a pret-ty moo;
nan, nan here, and a nan, nan there, Here a nan, there a nan, here a pret-ty nan;
D.C.
Six pret-ty maids come and gang a-long o' me To the mer-ry green fields and the farm - yard.
D.C.

Other verses may be added e.g. sheep (baa baa), hens (cluck cluck).

28. ANDULKO

Czech folk-song ('Andulko Šafárova'), translated by Roger Fiske.
'Andulko' means 'Little angel.'

Moderato
VOICE
PIANO
mp
Con Ped.
1. An- dul - ko, are you at home, my dear? There's no time to wait, All your fat geese have es-caped, I fear; They ran through the gate.
2. I'd call them in on- ly I'm a- -fraid My mis-tress would wake. She sleeps so light - ly, and you can guess The trou - ble she'd make.
mf
All your geese in the corn! Call them in ere it's morn.
Oh, how cross she can be! She would soon pu - nish me.
An-dul- ko, quick-ly come down, my dear, Be-fore it's too late.
I can't leave my lit - tle bed - room here Be-fore the day-break.
D.C.

29. SCRAPING UP SAND

American folk-song

Lightly
VOICE
PIANO
p
1. Scrap-ing up sand in the bot-tom of the sea,
2. Black those shoes and make them shine,
Con Ped.
Shi-loh, Shi-loh,
Scrap-ing up sand in the bot-tom of the sea,
Black those shoes and make them shine,
Shi-loh, Li-za Jane.
mp
Oh, how I love her, Oh, Li-za
Jane, Oh, how I love her, Good-bye, Li-za Jane.
D.C.

3 Hump-backed mule I'm/bound to ride,

4 Hopped up a chicken and he/flew upstairs.

30. THE SHEPHERDESS

French folk-song (*'Il était une bergère'*), translated by J. Wishart

Simply
mp
VOICE
PIANO
mp
1. A shep-herd-ess was watch - ing,
2. A cheese she made one morn - ing,
Ding-
-dong, ding-dong, ting-a - ling, ding-dong,
A shep-herd-ess was watch - ing Her
A cheese she made one morn - ing; Her
flock the whole day long, ding-dong, Her flock the whole day long.
churn turned to a song, ding-dong, Her churn turned to a song.
D.C.
D.C.

3 Her pussy-cat lay winking,
His thoughts, I fear, were wrong.

4 "If paw should touch, I'm whacking,
With rod both stout and strong."

5 Not paw, but neck came stretching,
To puss those lips belong.

6 The shepherdess was angry,
Poor puss! he died ere long.

31. THE LITTLE BOY AND THE SHEEP

French folk-song (*'Je suis un petit garçon'*); English words by James Taylor

Moderato
mp
VOICE
PIANO
mp
1. La - zy sheep, pray tell me why In the plea - sant fields you lie, Eat - ing grass and dai - sies white From the morn - ing to the night.
2. Nay, my lit - tle mas - ter, nay, Do not serve me so, I pray; Don't you see the wool that grows On my back to make your clothes?
D.C.
Ev - 'ry-thing can some-thing do, But what kind of use are you?
Cold, ah, ve - ry cold you'd be, If you had not wool from me.
D.C.

3 True, it seems a pleasant thing,
Eating daisies in the Spring;
But what chilly nights I pass
On the cold and dewy grass,
And sometimes the ground is bare,
I can't find food anywhere.

4 Then the farmer comes at last,
When the merry Spring is past;
Cuts my woolly fleece away
For your coat on wintry day;
Little master, this is why
In the pleasant fields I lie.

32. BOBBY SHAFTO

Northumbrian folk-song

Brightly
VOICE
PIANO
mp
Bob-by Shaf-to's gone to sea,– Sil-ver buck-les on his knee;– He'll come back and mar-ry me,– Bon-ny Bob-by Shaf - to.
1. Bob-by Shaf-to's bright and fair, Comb-ing down his yel - low hair; He's my ain for ev - er - mair, Bon-ny Bob-by Shaf - to.
2. Bob-by Shaf-to's tall and slim, Al-ways dress'd so neat and trim; Las-sies they all keek at him, Bon-ny Bob-by Shaf - to.
1
2
Bob-by Shaf-to's been to sea,– Sil-ver buck-les on his knee;– He's come back and mar-ried me,– Bon-ny Bob-by Shaf-to.

33. THE COBBLER AND THE CROW

American folk-song

Briskly
VOICE
PIANO
mp
1. There was a mer - ry cob - bler, bu - sy as a bee,
2. "Now, wife, you go and drive yon dusk - y crow a-way,
Li - ly, li - ly, li - ly, li - ly, Li - - do.
mf
When an old black crow came and perched up-on the tree.
Or he'll perch and croak till the end - ing of the day."
With its Qua! Qua! Qua! Qua!
Li - ly, li - ly, li - ly, li - ly, Li - - do.
D.C.

3 The cobbler's wife she tried to drive away the crow,
But the more she tried, the more he wouldn't go.

4 Then spoke the merry cobbler at the close of day:
"If the crow won't go, we shall have to let him stay."

34. THE BARNYARD SONG

American folk-song

Clearly
VOICE
PIANO
mp
mp
1. I had a cat and the cat pleased me. I fed my cat by yonder tree: Cat goes fid-dle-de-fee.
Verses 2-9
2. I had a hen and the hen pleased me. I fed my hen by yon-der tree:
Verses 2-9
*
Hen goes chimmy chuck, chimmy chuck, Cat goes fid-dle-de-fee.
*

3 Duck—quack, quack, quack, quack

4 Goose—swishy, swashy, swishy, swashy

5 Sheep—baa, baa, baa, baa

6 Pig—griffy, gruffy, griffy, gruffy

7 Cow—moo, moo, moo, moo

8 Horse—neigh, neigh, neigh, neigh

9 Dog—bow, wow, bow, wow

* Repeat this bar as required, adding the 'sounds' of a new animal in each verse.

35. TURN THE GLASSES OVER

American singing game

Moderato
mp
VOICE
PIANO
Con Ped.
I've been to Har-lem, I've been to Do-ver,
I've tra-velled this wide world all o-ver, O-ver, o-ver,
three times o-ver, Drink what you have to drink and turn the glas-ses o-ver.
Sail-ing east, sail-ing west, Sail-ing o-ver the o-cean,
Bet-ter watch out when the boat be-gins to rock, Or you'll lose your girl in the o-cean.

36. GREEN GROW THE LEAVES

Northumbrian folk-song

Brightly
mp
VOICE
PIANO
mp
Green grow the leaves up-on the
haw-thorn tree; Some they grow high and some they grow
lee. But the wrang-lers and the jang-lers, they nev-er can a-
-gree, And the bur-then of my song goes mer-ri-ly.

mf
Mer - ri - ly we go, boys, mer - ri - ly we go, And the
mf
bur - then of my song goes— mer - ri - ly.
FINE
FINE
p
Twen - ty, nine - teen, eigh - teen, seven - teen, six - teen, fif - teen, four - teen, thir - teen,
p
twelve, e - lev - en, ten, nine, eight, seven, six, five,— four,— three,
rit. f
D.S. al fine
D.S. al fine
rit. f

37. OH, SUSANNA

Tune and words by Stephen C. Foster

Lightly
mp
VOICE
PIANO
mp
1. I _ came from A - la - ba - ma with my ban - jo on my knee. I'm _ goin' to Loui - si - a - na now, my true love for to see. It _ rained all night the day I left, the wea - ther it was dry; The _ sun so hot I froze to death; Su - san - na, don't you cry.
2. I _ had a dream the oth - er night, when ev - 'ry - thing was still, I _ thought I saw Su - san - na dear a - com - ing down the hill. The _ buck - wheat cake was in her mouth, a tear was in her eye; Says _ I, "I'm com - ing from the south; Su - san - na, don't you cry."
mf
Oh, Su - san - na, Oh
mp
mf
mp

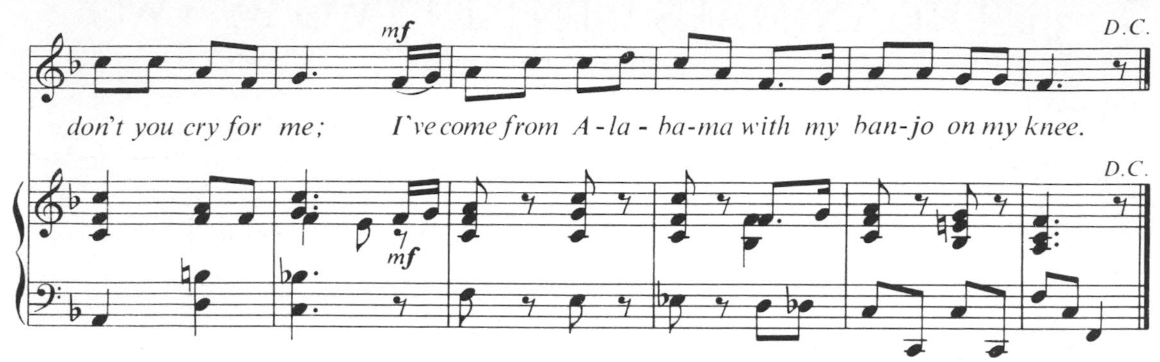

mf
D.C.
don't you cry for me; I've come from A-la-ba-ma with my ban-jo on my knee.
D.C.
mf

38. SHENANDOAH

American sea shanty

With movement

VOICE

PIANO

mp

1. O Shen-an-doah, I long to hear you,
2. O Shen-an-doah, I love your daugh-ter,

mf

A - way, you roll-ing ri - ver!

mp

O Shen-an-doah, I long to hear you;
She sent me sail - ing 'cross the wa - ter;

mf

A - way, I'm bound to go 'Cross the wide Mis - sou - ri.

D.S.

3 O Shenandoah, I took a notion,
Away, you rolling river!
To sail across the briny ocean;
Away, I'm bound etc.

4 O Shenandoah, I long to hear you,
Away, you rolling river!
O Shenandoah, I long to hear you;
Away, I'm bound etc.

39. THE ANIMALS WENT IN TWO BY TWO

English traditional song

Firmly
mp
VOICE
PIANO
mp
1. The an - i - mals went in
2. The an - i - mals went in
two by two
three by three
Hur - rah!
Hur - rah!
The an - i - mals went in
The an - i - mals went in
two by two
three by three
Hur - rah!
Hur - rah!
The an - i - mals went in
The an - i - mals went in
two by two, The el - e - phant and the kan - ga - roo,
three by three, The wasp, the ant and the bum - ble - bee,
And they

D.C.
all went in-to the ark For to get out of the rain.
D.C.

* ♮ last time only

3 The animals went in four by four
Hurrah! hurrah!
The animals went in four by four
Hurrah! hurrah!
The animals went in four by four:
The great hippopotamus stuck in the door,
And they all etc.

4 The animals went in five by five
Hurrah! hurrah!
The animals went in five by five
Hurrah! hurrah!
The animals went in five by five:
By eating each other they kept alive,
And they all etc.

5 The animals went in six by six
Hurrah! hurrah!
The animals went in six by six
Hurrah! hurrah!
The animals went in six by six:
They turned out the monkey because of his tricks,
And they all etc.

6 The animals went in seven by seven
Hurrah! hurrah!
The animals went in seven by seven
Hurrah! hurrah!
The animals went in seven by seven:
The little pig thought he was going to heaven,
And they all etc.

40. LI'L LIZA JANE

American traditional song

Lightly
VOICE
PIANO
mp
1. I know a gal that you don't know,
2. Li - za Jane looks good to me,
Li'l Li - za Jane,
'Way down south in Bal - ti - mo,'
Sweet - est one I ev - er see,
Li'l Li - za Jane,
mf
Oh, E - li - za, li'l Li - za
Jane,
p
Oh, E - li - za, li'l Li - za Jane!
D.C.

3 Where she lives the posies grow,
Chickens roun' the kitchen do'.

4 What do I care how far we roam?
Where she's at is home, sweet home.

41. SACRAMENTO

Sea shanty

VOICE
PIANO
1. A - round Cape Horn we're bound to go,
2. A - round Cape Horn in the month of May,
3. To the Sac - ra - men-to we're bound a-way,
Sac-ra-
- men-to, Sac-ra-men - to,
A - round Cape Horn thro' sleet and snow
A - round Cape Horn is a very long way
To the Sac- ra - men- to's a long, long way.
To the
banks o' Sac- ra-men-to. Blow, boys, blow, for Cal - i-for- nia, O! There's
plen- ty o' gold so I've been told On the banks o' Sac - ra-men - to.
D.C.
D.C.

42. SALLY BROWN

American sea shanty.
'Mulatter' is 'mulatto', of mixed white and negro blood.

Boldly
VOICE
PIANO
mf
1. Sal - ly Brown she's a bright mu - lat - ter,
2. Sev'n long years I__ court - ed Sal - ly,
Way - ay - y roll and go;
She drinks rum and chews ter - bac-cer,
Sev'n long years I court - ed Sal - ly,
mp
Verses 1 to 4
D.S.
Last verse
Spend my mo-ney on Sal - ly Brown.
Spend my mo-ney on Sal - ly Brown.

3 Sally Brown she has a daughter,
Way-ay-y roll and go;
Sent me sailing 'cross the water,
Spend my money on Sally Brown.

4 Sally lives on the old plantation,
Way-ay-y roll and go;
She's a girl of the Wild Goose nation,
Spend my money on Sally Brown.

5 Sally Brown she's a bright mulatter,
Way-ay-y roll and go;
She drinks rum and chews terbaccer,
Spend my money on Sally Brown.

43. THE SMUGGLER'S SONG

Old English tune, with words by Huw Lewis

Moderato
VOICE
PIANO
mp
1. See at the wa - ter's edge, Where the beach is
2. Hark! a warn-ing pis - tol shot: The Ex-cise-men are
san - dy; Four and twen - ty jol - ly lads, Land - ing kegs of
rid - ing! Off darts the French - ies' boat, Through the wat - er
p
bran - dy. Hear their lead - er soft - ly swear: "Ea - sy with the bar - rels there!
glid - ing. Out goes ev - 'ry lan - tern light, Fig - ures creep off through the night,
cresc.
Roll them up the beach with care! And keep your pis - tols hand - y!"
Roll the bar - rels out of sight! The smug - glers are in hid - ing!
D. C.

44. RIO GRANDE

British sea shanty.

The Rio Grande is a river in Brazil, not the North American river.

Moderato
VOICE
PIANO
mp
mf
1. Oh, where are you go - ing, my pret-ty maid?
may I go with you, my pret-ty maid?
Oh, Ri - o!
"I'm go - ing a - milk - ing, Sir," she said,
"You're kind - ly wel - come, Sir," she said,
But we're
bound for the Ri - o Grande. Then a - way, love, a - way,
'Way, for Ri - o, So fare you well, my bon-ny young girl, For we're

3 Oh, what is your father, my pretty maid?
Oh, Rio,
"My father's a farmer, Sir," she said,
But we're bound etc.

4 Oh, pray will you marry me, my pretty maid?
Oh, Rio,
"I will if you wish, kind Sir," she said,
But we're bound etc.

5 Oh, what is your fortune, my pretty maid?
Oh, Rio,
"My face is my fortune, Sir," she said,
But we're bound etc.

6 Oh, then I can't marry you, my pretty maid,
Oh, Rio,
"Oh, nobody asked you, Sir," she said,
But we're bound etc.

45. SWEET NIGHTINGALE

English folk-song

Flowing
VOICE
PIANO
1. My sweet-heart, come a - -long, Don't you hear the fond song, The sweet notes of the night - in-gale flow? Don't you
2. Pret-ty Bet - ty, don't fail, For I'll car- ry your pail Safe home to your cot as we go. You shall
hear the fond tale of the sweet night-in-gale, As she sings in the val- ley be - low,
As she sings in the val - ley be - low(?)
D.S.
D.S.

3 "Pray let me alone,
I have hands of my own,
Along with you, Sir, I'll not go
For to hear the fond tale" etc.

4 Pray sit yourself down
With me on the ground,
On this bank where the primroses grow,
You shall hear the fond tale etc.

5 The couple agreed
To be married with speed,
And soon to the church they did go.
No more is she afraid
For to walk in the shade
Or to sit in those valleys below,
Or to sit in those valleys below.

46. LEAVE HER, JOHNNY

British sea shanty

Not too fast
VOICE
PIANO
mp
1. I thought I heard the skip - per say,
2. The work was hard and the pas - sage long,
Leave her, John - ny, leave her!
"To - mor - row you will get your pay:"
The seas were high and the gales were strong,
It's time for us to leave her.
D.C.

3 The food was bad and the wages low,
But now ashore again we'll go.

4 The sails are furled and our work is done,
And now on shore we'll have some fun.

47. PRETTY POLLY OLIVER

17th-century English song

Moderato
VOICE
PIANO
mp
1. As pret-ty Pol - ly O - li-ver lay mus-ing in bed, A com - i - cal fan - cy came in - to her head: "Nor fa - ther nor moth - er shall make me false prove, I'll 'list for a sol - dier and fol - low my love."
2. The drums they did beat and the trum-pets did blow When Pol - ly in un-i-form to the war she did go, Her lo - ver was wound-ed and fell by her side, And, as Pol - ly lift-ed him, she knew that he had died.
D.C.

3 Poor Polly sat crying, dead soldiers all around,
When up came the Captain, who said as he frowned:
"A soldier here weeping, a soldier afraid?"
"Oh, Sir! I'm no soldier," said Polly, "I'm a maid."

4 "A maid?" said the Captain, "then throw her in jail."
"Oh, no," pleaded Polly, who told her sad tale,
And when a great vic-t'ry had ended the strife
The Captain took Polly and made her his wife.

48. ROBIN ADAIR

Irish tune, with words attributed to Robert Burns

Fairly slowly
VOICE
PIANO
p
1. What's this dull town to me? Ro - bin's not near. What was't I wished to see, What wished to hear?
2. What made th'as - semb - ly shine? Ro - bin A - dair. What made the ball so fine? Ro - bin was there.
3. But now thou'rt cold to me, Ro - bin A - dair. But now thou'rt cold to me, Ro - bin A - dair.
mp
Where all the joy and mirth Made this town heav'n on earth?
What when the play was o'er, What made my heart so sore?
Yet he I loved so well Still in my heart shall dwell;
mf
Oh, they're all fled with thee, Ro - bin A - dair.
Oh, it was part - ing with Ro - bin A - dair.
Oh, I can ne'er for - get Ro - bin A - dair.
D.C.

49. O RARE TURPIN

English traditional song. The narrator is Turpin.

Moderato
VOICE
PIANO
mf
1. On Houn-slow Heath as I rode o'er, I spied a law-yer ri-ding be-fore. "Kind Sir," said I, "aren't you a-fraid Of Tur-pin, that mis-chiev-ous blade?"
2. Says Tur-pin, "He'll ne'er find me out. I've hid my mon-ey in my boot." The law-yer says, "There's none can find My gold stitched in my cape be-hind."
O rare Tur-pin he-ro, O rare Tur-pin, O.
D.C.

3 As they rode by the powder mill
Our Turpin bids him to stand still,
Says he, "Your cape I must cut off,
My mare she wants a saddle cloth."

4 This caused the lawyer much to fret
To think he was so fairly hit;
And Turpin robbed him of his store,
Because he knew he'd lie for more.

* ♮ last time only

50. THE LASS OF RICHMOND HILL

Tune by J. Hook, words by W. Upton.

The poem honours a 'lass' who lived in Richmond, Yorkshire.

Gently
mp
VOICE
PIANO
1. On Rich-mond Hill there lives a lass, More bright than May-day
2. How hap-py will the lo - ver be Who calls the maid his
morn, Whose charms all oth- er maids sur- pass, A rose with-out a thorn.
own, O may her choice be fixed on me, Mine's fixed on her a - lone.
mf
This
lass so neat, with smiles so sweet, Has won my right good will, I'd crowns re - sign to
call thee mine, Sweet lass of Rich-mond Hill; Sweet lass of Rich-mond Hill, Sweet
lass of Rich-mond Hill, I'd crowns re-sign to call thee mine, Sweet lass of Rich-mond Hill.
D.C.

51. THE LINCOLNSHIRE POACHER

English traditional song

Moderato
VOICE
PIANO
mf
mf
1. When I was bound_ ap-
2. As me and my___ com-
-pren - tice, in fam - ous Lin - coln - shire,___ Full well I served my
-pan - i-ons were set - ting of a snare,___ 'Twas then we spied the
mas - ter for more than sev - en year,___ Till I took up to
game-keep-er, for him we did_ not care,___ For we can wrestle and
poach - ing, as you shall quick- ly hear;
fight, my boys, and jump o'er an - y-where;
Oh! 'tis my de-light on a

f
shin - ing night in the sea - son of the year. Oh! 'tis
f
D.C.
my de-light on a shin - ing night in the sea - son of the year.
D.C.

3 As me and my companions were setting four or five,
And taking on 'em up again, we caught a hare alive,
We took the hare alive, my boys, and through the woods did steer;
Oh, 'tis my delight etc.

4 I took him on my shoulder, and then we trudgèd home,
We took him to a neighbour's house and sold him for a crown,
We sold him for a crown, my boys, I did not tell you where;
Oh, 'tis my delight etc.

5 Success to every gentleman who lives in Lincolnshire,
Success to every poacher who wants to sell a hare,
Bad luck to every gamekeeper who will not sell his deer;
Oh, 'tis my delight etc.

52. I'SE THE B'Y THAT BUILDS THE BOAT

Newfoundland folk-song

Moderato
VOICE
PIANO
mp
1. I'se the b'y that builds the boat,
2. Flour and crumbs to cover your fish,
I'se the b'y that sails her! I'se the b'y that catch-es the fish And
Cake and tea for sup - per, Cod fish in the spring o' the year
takes them home to Li - za.
Fried in ran-cid but - ter.
mf
Hip yer part - ner, Sal - ly Tib - bo, Hip yer part - ner,
Sal - ly Brown! *Fo - go, Twill-in-gate, More-ton's Har-bour, All a-round the cir - cle!
D.C.

3 I don't want your rancid fish,
That's no good for winter;
I could buy as good as that
Down in Bonavista.
Hip yer partner, etc.

4 I took Liza to a dance,
And faith, but she could travel!
Every step that she did take
Was up to her knees in gravel.
Hip yer partner, etc.

5 Susan White, she's out of sight,
Her petticoat wants a border;
Old Sam Oliver in the dark
He kissed her in the corner.
Hip yer partner, etc.

*The places mentioned are ports round Notre Dame Bay in N.E. Newfoundland.

53. JOHN BARLEYCORN

Somerset folk-song

Moderato
VOICE
PIANO
mp
1. There came three men from out the west Their
2. They took a plough and ploughed him in, Laid
vic - to - ry to try, And they have ta - ken a sol-emn oath John Bar - ley-corn should
clods up - on his head, And they have ta - ken a sol-emn oath John Bar - ley-corn is
die.
dead.
mf
Sing ri - fol - lol, the did-dle all the dee, Right fal-lee - ro - dee.
D.C.

3 So then he lay for three long weeks
Till dew from heaven did fall;
John Barleycorn sprang up again
And that surprised them all.

4 There he remained till midsummer
And looked both pale and wan,
For all he had a spikey beard
To show he was a man.

5 But soon men came with their sharp scythes
And chopped him to the knee;
They rolled and tied him by the waist
And served him barbarously.

54. HOPE, THE HERMIT

English 17th-century tune; words by John Oxenford

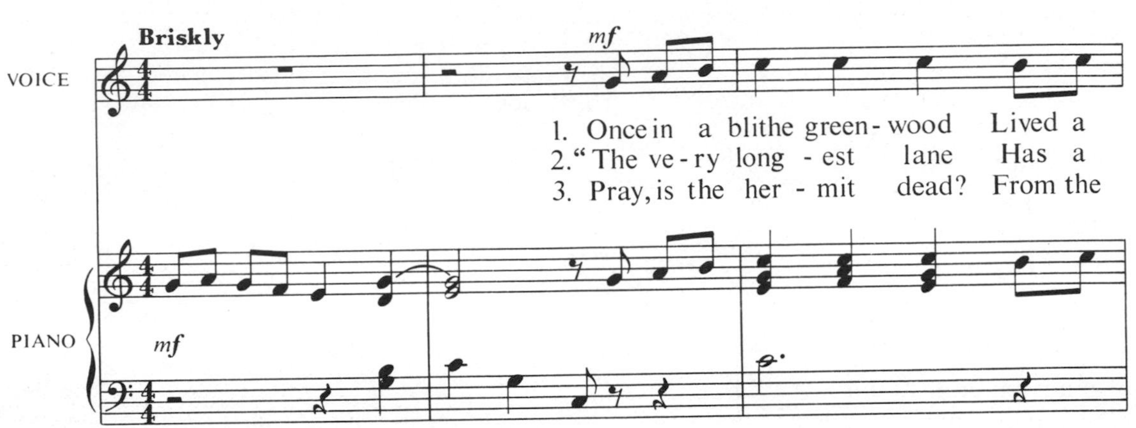
Briskly
mf
VOICE
PIANO
mf
1. Once in a blithe green-wood Lived a
2.“The ve-ry long-est lane Has a
3. Pray, is the her-mit dead? From the

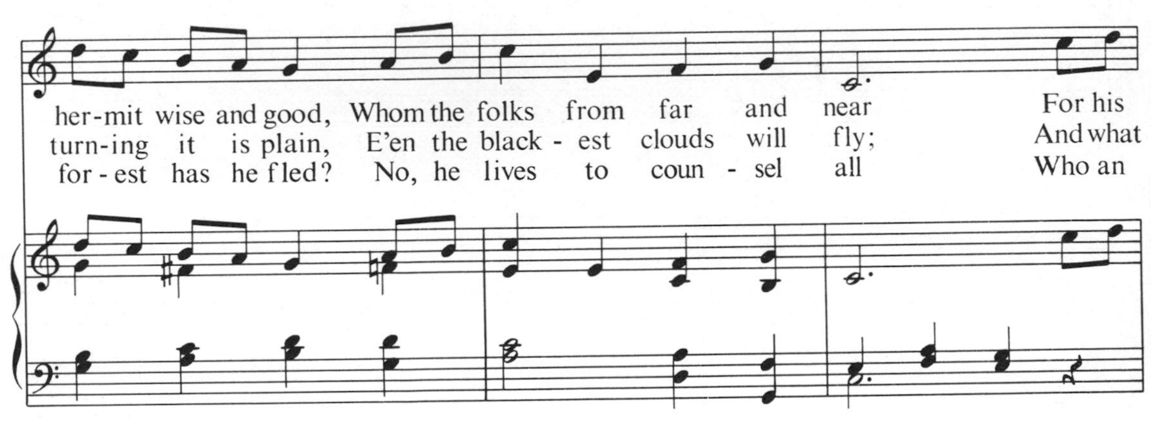
her-mit wise and good, Whom the folks from far and near For his
turn-ing it is plain, E'en the black-est clouds will fly; And what
for-est has he fled? No, he lives to coun-sel all Who an

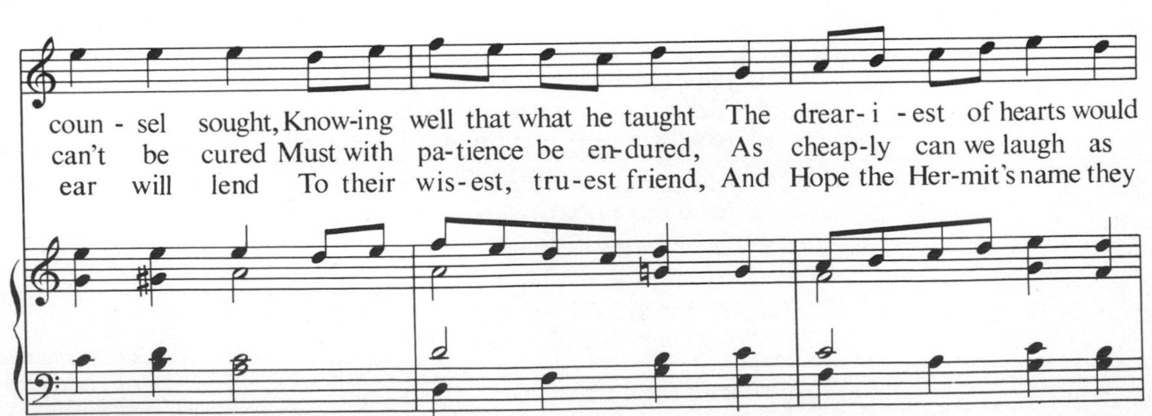
coun-sel sought, Know-ing well that what he taught The drear-i-est of hearts would
can't be cured Must with pa-tience be en-dured, As cheap-ly can we laugh as
ear will lend To their wis-est, tru-est friend, And Hope the Her-mit's name they

cheer. Though his hair was white His eye was clear and bright, And he
cry." And the peo - ple gazed, At words so deep, am - azed, While the
call; Still he sits, I ween, 'Mid bran-ches ev - er green, And
thus was ev - er wont to say:
sage went on to say:
cheer - ly you may hear him say:
"Though to care we are born, Yet the
dull - est morn Oft - en her - alds in the fair - est day,
Though to
care we are born, Yet the dull - est morn Oft - en her - alds in the fair - est day!"
f
D.C.
D.C.

55. HO-LA-HI

German folk-song, translated by Elizabeth Fiske

Lightly
VOICE
PIANO
mp
1. Lis-ten to the cheer-ful cry,
2. I - dle peo-ple ques-tion me,
3. Spite-ful peo-ple some-times hiss,
Ho- la - hi,
Is my sweet-heart pass - ing by?
ho - la - ho, What my true love's name can be,
No-thing good can come of this,
Ho - la - hi - a - ho!
mf
No, the voice fades down the street,
Let them won - der, let them tease,
She will ne - ver be your own,
Ho - la - hi, ho - la - ho,
f
D.S.
That was not my dar - ling sweet,
I shall love just as I please,
Yet do I love her a - lone,
Ho - la - hi - a - ho!

56. FISHERMAN'S NIGHT SONG

Irish folk-song, with words by L. A. G. Strong

Moderato
VOICE
PIANO
mp
1. In the calm hour of eve-ning When the sea-gulls fly slow To their rocks on the is-land And cry as they go, From each house on the head-land Lights be-gin to twin-kle in the gloom, And the pale cold world dwin-dles To a warm qui-et room.
2. Let us sit by the fire-side And re-mem-ber our friends. Each day ends in dark-ness But hope ne-ver ends. When the last shoal is ta-ken And the last boat comes to shore, We will all sing to-geth-er, Di-vi-ded no more.
mf
mp
D.C.

57. FAREWELL, MANCHESTER!

Tune by Rev. William Felton (1713-1769), and said to have been played when the Young Pretender's army left Manchester in 1747. Words by John Oxenford.

Not too slowly
VOICE
PIANO
p
1. Fare - well, Man-ches - ter! no-ble town, fare - well! Here with loy - al - ty ev - 'ry breast can swell:
2. Fare - well, Man-ches - ter! sad-ly I de - part, Tear - drops bo-ding-ly from their pri - son start;
cresc.
Where - so - e'er I roam, Here, as in a home,
Though I toil a - new Sha - dows to pur-sue,
dim.
Ev - er, dear Lan-ca-shire, My heart shall dwell.
Sha-dows vain— thou'lt re-main With - in my heart.
D.C.

58. FAITHFUL JOHNNY

Scottish traditional song

Gently
VOICE
PIANO
p
1. When will you come a - gain?
2. Then win-ter's wind will blow,
3. Then will you meet me here?
My_ faith-ful John-ny;
When will you come a - gain?
Then win-ter's wind will blow,
Then will you meet me here?
My_ faith-ful John-ny;
mf
When the corn is ga - ther-ed, When the leaves are wi - ther-ed,
Though the day be dark with drift, That I_ can - not see the_ lift,
Though the night were Hal - low - een, When the fear - ful sights are seen,
p
pp
I will come a-gain, My_ sweet and bon-ny, I will come a - gain._
D.C.

59. ELSIE MARLEY

Tune by Thomas Dunhill, with traditional English words

Merrily
VOICE
PIANO
mf
Do you ken El - sie Mar - ley, hon-ey, The wife that sells the bar - ley, hon-ey, The
wife that sells the bar - ley?
f
Do you ken El - sie, Do you ken El - sie,
Do you ken El - sie Mar - ley?
El - sie Mar - ley's grown so fine_ She

won't get up to feed the swine,_But lies in bed till eight or nine, And
sure - ly she_ does take her time.
p
Do you ken El - sie Mar - ley, hon-ey, The wife that sells the bar - ley, hon-ey, The
p
wife, the wife, the wife that sells the bar - ley?
f
f

60. EARLY ONE MORNING

English folk-song

Moderato
VOICE
PIANO
mp
mp
1. Ear - ly one morn - ing just as the sun was ri - sing, I heard a maid-en sing in the val - ley be - low:
2. "Gay is the gar - land and fresh are the ro - ses I've culled from the gar - den to bind on your brow:"
3. Thus sang the maid - en, her sor - rows be - wail - ing, Thus sang the poor maid in the val - ley be - low:
"Oh, don't de - ceive me, Oh, ne - ver leave me, How could you use a poor maid-en so?"
D.C.
D.C.

61. CAPTAIN MORGAN'S MARCH

Welsh folk-song, 'Rhyfelgyrch Capten Morgan'.
English version by J. B. P. Dobbs.

Boldly
VOICE
PIANO
mf
1. Men of Mor-gan-wg, rise a-gainst the foe!
2. Men of Mor-gan-wg, rise to li - ber-ty!
Send him hence or lay him low,
Cym - ru now shall soon be free,
Leave all your books, your
With her own lan - guage,
pas - ture and your plough;
sing - ing her own songs,
Gird on wea - pons, join us now.
Right - ing all her conq -'ror's wrongs.
f
D.C. v.2
Mor-gan calls you, bids you with him stand,
Drive the raid-ing Sa - xon from this fair land.

Pronunciation: *Morganwg* = Morganoog *Cymru* = Kumri

62. THE CUCKOO

Austrian folk-song, with words by Katherine F. Rohrbaugh

Simply
mp
VOICE
PIANO
Con Ped.
1. Oh, I went to Pe-ter's flow-ing spring Where the wa - ter's so good; And I heard there the cuck - oo As he called from the wood.
2. Af - ter East - er come sun - ny days That will melt all the snow; Then I'll mar - ry my maid - en fair: We'll be hap - py, I know.
3. When I've mar - ried my maid - en fair What then can I de - sire? Oh, a home for her ten - ding And some wood for the fire.
Ho - - li - - ah,
mf
Ho - le-rah-hi-hi-ah, Ho - le-rah ku-kuck, Ho - le-rah-hi-hi-ah, Ho - le-rah ku-kuck,
Ho - le-rah-hi-hi-ah, Ho - le-rah ku-kuck, Ho - le-rah-hi-hi-ah ho.
D.C.
D.C.

63. THE BRITISH GRENADIERS

English traditional song

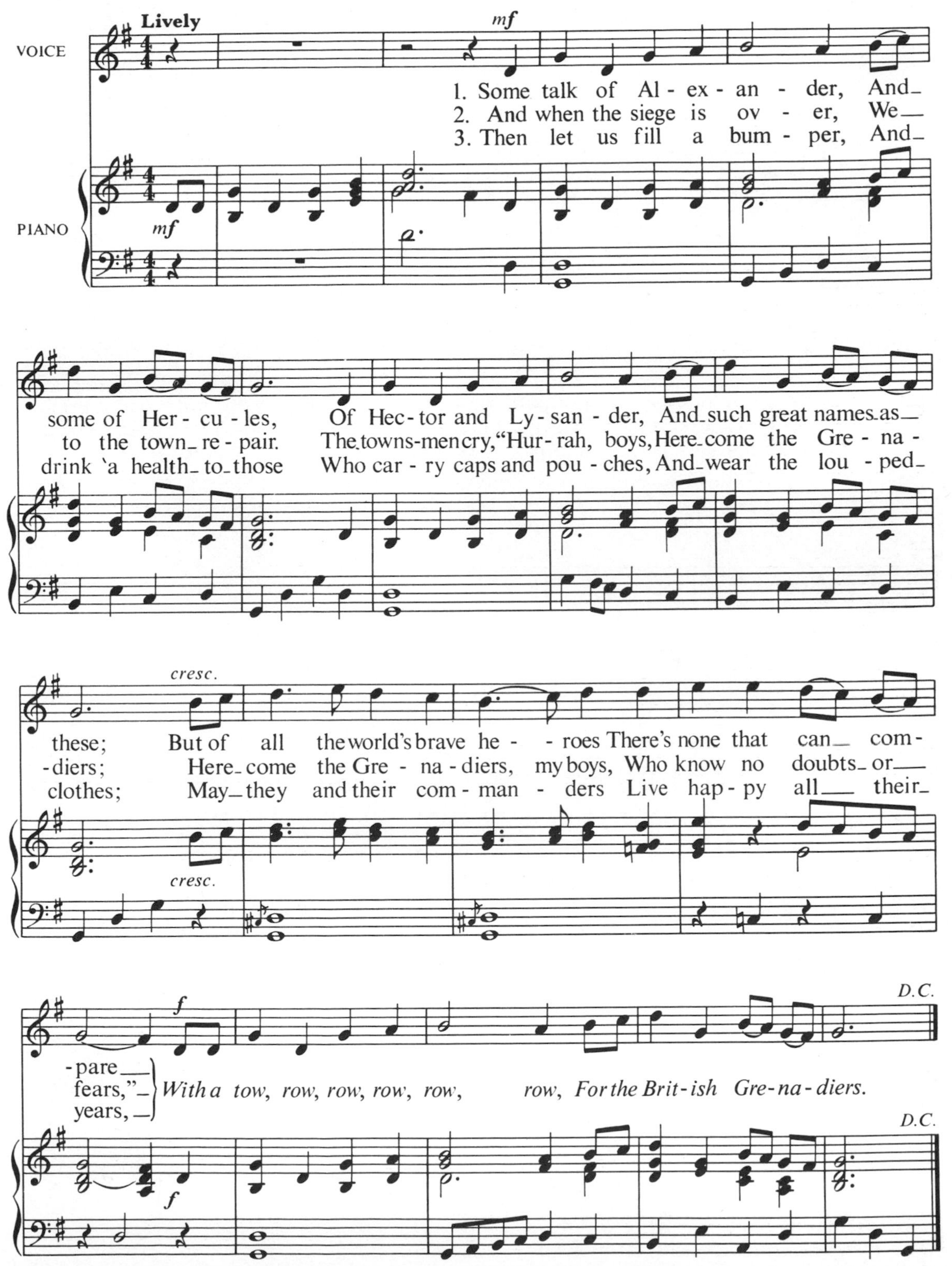
Lively
mf
VOICE
PIANO
1. Some talk of Al - ex - an - der, And_ some of Her - cu - les, Of Hec - tor and Ly - san - der, And_such great names_as_ these; But of all the world's brave he - - roes There's none that can_ com- -pare_
2. And when the siege is ov - er, We_ to the town_ re - pair. The_towns-men cry, "Hur - rah, boys, Here_come the Gre - na - -diers; Here_come the Gre - na - diers, my boys, Who know no doubts_ or_ fears,"_
3. Then let us fill a bum - per, And_ drink 'a health_ to_those Who car - ry caps and pou - ches, And_wear the lou - ped_ clothes; May_they and their com - man - ders Live hap - py all_ their_ years,_
With a tow, row, row, row, row, row, For the Brit - ish Gre - na - diers.
cresc.
f
D.C.

64. COCKLES AND MUSSELS

Irish traditional song

Simply
VOICE
PIANO
p
1. In Dub - lin's fair ci - ty, Where girls are so pret - ty, I first set my eyes on sweet Mol - ly Mal - one, As she wheeled her wheel - bar - row Through streets broad and nar - row, Cry - ing,
2. She was a fish - mong - er, But sure 'twas no won - der, For so were her fath - er and moth - er be - fore, And they each wheeled their bar - row Through streets broad and nar - row, Cry - ing,
3. She died of a fev - er, And no one could save her, And that was the end of sweet Mol - ly Mal - one, But her ghost wheels her bar - row Through streets broad and nar - row, Cry - ing,
"Cock - les and mus - sels! A - live, a - live oh!
"Cock - les and mus - sels! A - live, a - live oh!
"Cock - les and mus - sels! A - live, a - live oh!
mf
A - live, a - live oh! A -

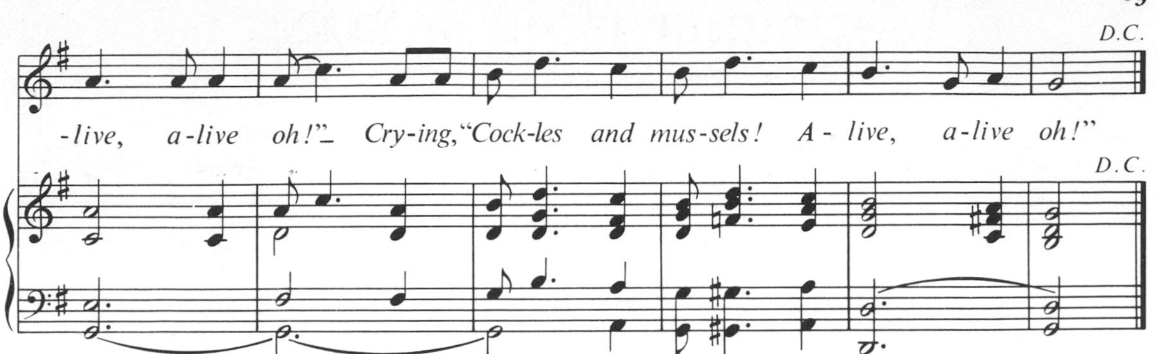
D.C.
-live, a-live oh!"– Cry-ing, "Cock-les and mus-sels! A - live, a-live oh!"
D.C.

65. BARBARA ALLEN

English traditional song

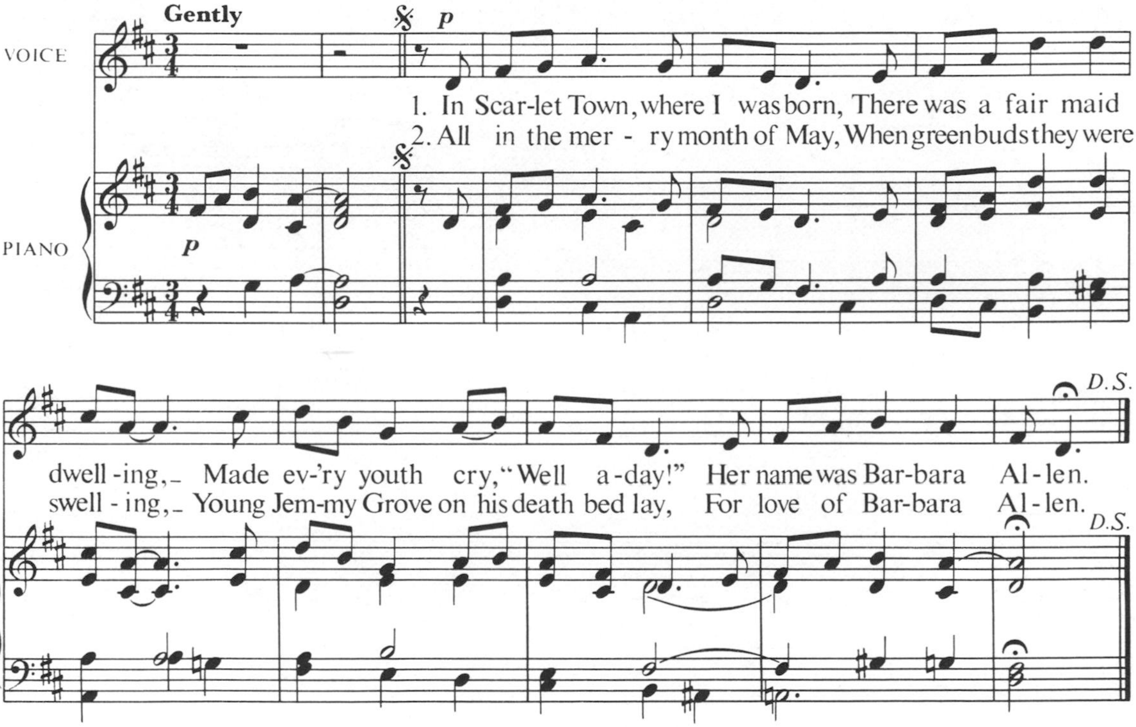

Gently

VOICE

PIANO

p

1. In Scar-let Town, where I was born, There was a fair maid dwell-ing,– Made ev-'ry youth cry, "Well a-day!" Her name was Bar-bara Al-len.
2. All in the mer - ry month of May, When green buds they were swell - ing,– Young Jem-my Grove on his death bed lay, For love of Bar-bara Al-len.

D.S.

3 So slowly, slowly she came up,
And slowly she came nigh him;
And all she said, when there she came:
"Young man, I think you're dying."

4 When he was dead and laid in grave,
Her heart was struck with sorrow;
"O mother, mother, make my bed,
For I shall die tomorrow!"

5 "Farewell," she said, "ye maidens all,
And shun the fault I fell in;
Henceforth take warning by the fall
Of cruel Barbara Allen."

66. CHARLIE IS MY DARLING

Scottish traditional tune, with words by Lady Nairne

Firmly
VOICE
PIANO
mp
Char-lie is m' dar - ling, m' dar - ling, m' dar - ling, Char- lie is m' dar - ling, the young Chev-a-lier.
mf
1. 'Twas on a Mon - day morn - ing Right ear - ly in the year, When Char - lie came to our town, The young Chev - a-lier,
2. As he came march-ing up the street, The pipes played loud and clear, And all the folks came run - ning out To meet the Chev - a-lier,
Oh!
D. S. for vv. 2, 3, 4.

After v. 4
mp
Char - lie is m' dar - ling, m' dar - ling, m' dar - ling,
After v. 4
mp
Char - lie is m' dar - ling, the young Chev - a - lier.

3 Wi' Hieland bonnets on their heads,
    And claymores bright and clear,
They came to fight for Scotland's right,
    And for the Chevalier.
        Oh! Charlie etc.

4 They've left their bonnie Hieland hills,
    Their wives and *children dear,
To draw the sword for Scotland's Lord,
    The young Chevalier.
        Oh! Charlie etc.

*or 'bairnies'

67. CADER IDRIS

Welsh folk-song, with words by Jacqueline Froom.
'Cader Idris' is the name of a mountain.

Gently
VOICE
mp
1. Light-heart - ed I stroll through the
2. Light-foot - ed I leap down the
PIANO
mp
Vale of Llan - goll - en, And climb the steep moun - tain, ad -
side of the moun - tain, My heart beat - ing fas - ter with
- mir - ing the view. All round me the moun - tains roll
thoughts of the past: How hap - py my life in that
on - ward and on - ward, Till dis - tance has changed all their
cot - tage be - low me, How hap - py the years that raced

mf
green in - to blue. I see the clear streams tum - bling down the steep-
on - ward so fast! I lived in that cot - tage with fa - ther and
mf
hill - side, And wa - ter - falls spill - ing their mist from a
mo - ther, And sis - ters and bro - thers were gath - ered a -
mp
height; I see a white cot - tage be - low by the
-round. But now all for - sa - ken, for - lorn and de -
mp
D.C.
birch - grove, And mem - 'ries of child - hood come shin - ing and bright.
-ser - ted, The cot - tage is crum - bling, and this - tles a - bound.
D.C.

68. BLOW AWAY THE MORNING DEW

Somerset folk-song

Moderato
mp
VOICE
PIANO
1. Up-on the sweet-est sum-mer-time In the mid-dle of the morn, A pret-ty dam-sel I es-pied, The fair-est ev-er born.
2. She gath-ered to her love-ly flowers And spent her time in sport, As if in pret-ty Cu-pid's bowers She dai-ly did re-sort.
mf
And sing blow a-way the morn-ing dew, the dew, and the dew, Blow a-way the morn-ing dew, How sweet the winds do blow.
D.C.

3 The yellow cowslip by the brim,
The daffodil as well,
The timid primrose, pale and trim,
The pretty snowdrop bell.
And sing etc.

4 She's gone with all those flowers sweet
Of white and red and blue,
And unto me about my feet
Is only left the rue.
And sing etc.

69. AFTON WATER

Scottish traditional tune, with words by Robert Burns

Simply
VOICE
PIANO
p
1. Flow gen - tly, sweet_ Af - ton, a - -
2. Thou stock - dove, whose_ ech - o re - -
- mong thy green_ braes,_ Flow gen - tly, I'll_ sing_ thee a__
- sounds through the__ glen,__ Ye wild, whist - ling_ black-birds in__
mp
song in_ thy_praise; My_ Ma - ry's_ a - sleep by thy mur-mur - ing_
yon thorn-y__ den, Thou green - cres - ted_ lap-wing, thy scream-ing for -
stream,_ Flow gen - tly, sweet_ Af - ton, di - sturb not_ her_ dream.
-bear, __ I charge you di - sturb_ not my_ slum - ber - ing_ fair.
D.C.
D.C.

70. THE ASH GROVE

Welsh traditional tune, with words by Thomas Oliphant

Gently
VOICE
PIANO
1. Down yon - der green val - ley where stream - lets me - an - der, When twi - light is fa - ding, I pen - sive - ly rove; Or at the bright noon-tide, in sol - i - tude wan - der A - mid the dark shades of the lone - ly Ash
2. Still glows the bright sun - shine o'er val - ley and moun - tain, Still war - bles the black - bird its notes from the tree; Still trem - bles the moon-beam on stream - let and foun - tain, But what are the beau - ties of na - ture to

mp
Grove. 'Twas there, while the black - bird was cheer - ful - ly
me? With sor - row, deep sor - row, my bo - som is
mp
sing - ing, I first met that dear one, the joy of my
la - den, All day I go mourn - ing in search of my
p
heart! A - round us for glad - ness the blue - bells were
love; Ye ech - oes! oh tell me, where is the sweet
p
ring - ing; Ah! then lit - tle thought I how soon we should part.
mai - den? "She sleeps 'neath the green turf down by the Ash Grove."
D.C.
D.C.

71. A-ROVING

English sea shanty

Moderato
VOICE
PIANO
mp
1. In Am-ster-dam there lived a maid, Mark well what I do say; In Am-ster-dam there lived a maid, And she was mis-tress of her trade,
2. Her cheeks were red, her eyes were brown, Mark well what I do say; Her cheeks were red, her eyes were brown, Her hair so black was hang-ing down,
3. I put my arm a-round her waist, Mark well what I do say; I put my arm a-round her waist, Says she, "Young man, you're in great haste!"
mf
I'll go no more a-rov-ing with you, fair maid.
A-rov-ing, a-rov-ing, Since rov-ing's been my

D.C.
ru - i - in, I'll go no more a - rov - ing with you, fair maid.
D.C.

72. GOLDEN SLUMBERS

English 17th-century song

Not too slowly

VOICE

PIANO

p

1. Gold - en slum - bers kiss your eyes,
2. Care you know not, there - fore sleep,

Smiles a - wake you when you rise;
While I o'er you watch do keep;

Sleep, pret - ty maid - en,
Sleep, pret - ty darl - ing,

do not cry, *p* And I will sing a lul - la - by.
do not cry, And I will sing a lul - la - by.

D.C.

D.C.

73. THE TREE IN THE WOOD

Somerset folk-song

Briskly
mp
VOICE
PIANO
mp
1. All in — a — wood there grew a tree, The
fin - est — tree you ev-er did see, And the green leaves grew a -
- round, a-round, a-round, And the green leaves grew a - round.
2. And
on — this — tree there was a limb, The fin - est — limb you ev-er did see, The

limb was on the tree, The tree was in the wood,— And the green leaves grew a-
- round, a-round, a-round, And the green leaves grew a- round. 3. And -round.
Verses 3 to 9
Verses 2 to 8
D.S.
Last time
Verses 3 to 9
Verses 2 to 8
D.S.
Last time

* This bar is sung twice in the 3rd verse, three times in the 4th verse etc.

3 And ON this limb there was a branch,
The finest branch you ever did see,
(*to 3 opposite*)

4 And ON this branch there was a nest,
The finest nest *etc.* (*to 4*)

5 And IN this nest there was an egg,
The finest egg *etc.* (*to 5*)

6 And IN this egg there was a yolk,
The finest yolk *etc.* (*to 6*)

7 And IN this yolk there was a bird,
The finest bird *etc.* (*to 7*)

8 And ON this bird there was a wing,
The finest wing *etc.* (*to 8*)

9 And ON this wing there was a feather,
The finest feather *etc.* (*to 9*)

9 The feather was ON the wing,
8 The wing was ON the bird,
7 The bird was IN the yolk,
6 The yolk was IN the egg,
5 The egg was IN the nest,
4 The nest was ON the branch,
3 The branch was ON the limb,
2 The limb was ON the tree,
1 The tree was IN the wood,
And the green leaves etc.

74. GREEN GROW THE RUSHES, HO!

English traditional song

Moderato
mf
VOICE
Start all verses here
I'll sing you one- two- three- etc. ho! Green grow the rush-es, ho! What is your one- two- three- etc. ho?
First verse to 1
Second verse to 2
Third verse to 3
Fourth verse to 4
Verses five to twelve to 5
PIANO
mf
1
D.C.
2
One is one and all a-lone and ev-er more shall be so. Two, two the li-ly-white boys,
cloth-ed all in green_ ho, One is one and all a-lone and ev-er more shall be so.
(Fine) D.C.
3
Back to 2
4
Back to 3
Three, three the ri - vals, Four for the Gos-pel mak-ers,

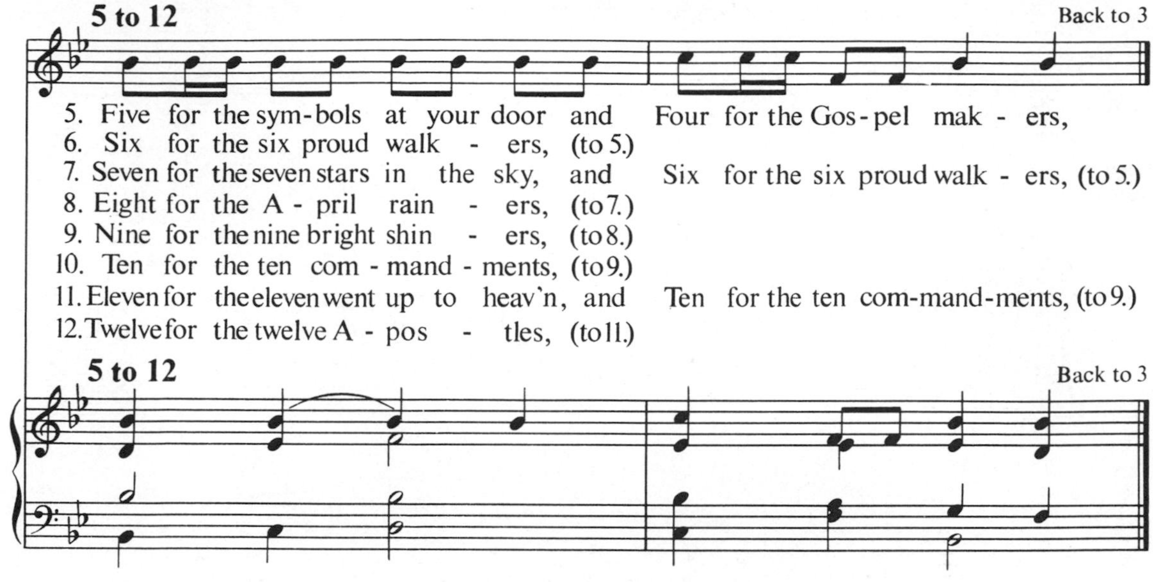
5 to 12
Back to 3
5. Five for the sym-bols at your door and Four for the Gos-pel mak - ers,
6. Six for the six proud walk - ers, (to 5.)
7. Seven for the seven stars in the sky, and Six for the six proud walk - ers, (to 5.)
8. Eight for the A - pril rain - ers, (to 7.)
9. Nine for the nine bright shin - ers, (to 8.)
10. Ten for the ten com - mand - ments, (to 9.)
11. Eleven for the eleven went up to heav'n, and Ten for the ten com-mand-ments, (to 9.)
12. Twelve for the twelve A - pos - tles, (to 11.)
5 to 12
Back to 3

There is no definitive explanation of this song, but the following are put forward as suggestions:

1. The Almighty
2. Christ and John the Baptist
3. The persons of the Trinity, or perhaps the Three Wise Men
4. Matthew, Mark, Luke and John
5. A five-pointed figure to ward off evil spirits
6. "Walkers" may have been originally "waters", meaning the six pots of water turned to wine
7. Charles's Wain—a group of stars
8. The eight saved in the Ark
9. Angels
10. The Ten Commandments
11. The Apostles, excluding Judas
12. The Apostles, including Judas

75. MARCHING THROUGH GEORGIA

Tune and words by Henry C. Work (American Civil War song)

Moderato
VOICE
PIANO
mf
1. Bring the good old bu - gle, boys, we'll
2. How the dark- ies shout - ed when they
sing an-oth-er song, Sing it with a spi-rit that will start the world a-long,
heard the joy-ful sound, How the tur-keys gob-bled which our Comm-iss- a - ry found;
Sing it as we used to sing it fif - ty thou-sand strong,
How the sweet po- ta-toes ev-en star-ted from the ground,
While we were march - ing through
Geor - gia. Hur-rah! hur-rah! we bring the Jub-i-lee! Hur-
f

-rah! hur-rah! the flag that makes you free! So we sang the cho-rus from At-

D.C.
-lan - ta to the sea, While we were march - ing through Geor - gia!
D.C.

3 Yes, and there were Union men who wept with joyful tears,
When they saw the honoured flag they had not seen for years;
Hardly could they be restrained from breaking into cheers,
While we were etc.

4 "Sherman's dashing Yankee boys will never reach the coast,"
So the saucy rebels said, and 'twas a handsome boast;
Had they not forgot, alas, to reckon with the host,
While we were etc.

5 So we made a thoroughfare for freedom and her train,
Sixty miles in latitude, three hundred to the main;
Treason fled before us, for resistance was in vain,
While we were etc.

76. JOHN BROWN'S BODY

March song of the American Civil War

77. JENNIE JENKINS

American singing game

Merrily

VOICE

PIANO

mp

1. O will you wear white, O my dear, O my dear? O will you wear white, Jen-nie Jen-kins? I won't wear white, for the col-our's too bright,
2. O will you wear red, O my dear, O my dear? O will you wear red, Jen-nie Jen-kins? I won't wear red, it's the col-our of my head,

I'll buy me a fol-di-rol-dy, til-di-tol-dy, seek a dou-ble, use a cause-a-roll to bind me.

mf *Roll, roll, roll, Jen-nie Jen-kins,*

Verses 1, 2, 3: *roll.—* *D.C.*

v. 4: *roll.—* *f* *roll!*

f *staccato* *mp* *mf*

3 O will you wear green?
I won't wear green, it's a shame to be seen.

4 O will you wear blue?
I won't wear blue, I'd be just like you.

78. CAMPTOWN RACES

Tune and words by Stephen C. Foster

Briskly
VOICE
PIANO
mf
1. The Camp-town la - dies sing this song,
2. The long-tail filly and the big black hoss,
f
Doo - dah! doo - dah! The Camp-town race-track five miles long,
Doo - dah! doo - dah! They fly the track an' they both cut a-cross,
Oh! doo - dah day! I come down there wid my hat caved in,
Oh! doo - dah day! The blind hoss sticking in a big mud hole,
Doo - dah! doo - dah! I go back home wid a pocket full of tin,
Doo - dah! doo - dah! Can't touch the bottom wid a ten - foot pole,

f
Oh! doo - dah day!
Oh! doo - dah day!
Gwine to run all night! Gwine to run all
f
D. C.
day! I'll_ bet my mo-ney on the bob- tail nag, Some - bo-dy bet on the bay.
D. C.

3 Old muley cow come on the track,
The bobtail fling her over his back,
Then fly along like a railroad car,
And run a race wid a shootin' star,
Oh! Doodah day!
Gwine to run etc.

4 Oh, see them flyin' on a ten-mile heat
Around the race-track then repeat,
I win my money on the bob-tail nag,
I keep my money in an old tow bag,
Oh! Doodah day!
Gwine to run etc.

79. YE BANKS AND BRAES

Scottish traditional tune, with words by Robert Burns

Not too slowly
VOICE
PIANO
p
1. Ye banks and braes_o' bon-nie Doon, How can_ye bloom sae
2. Oft hae I roved_by bon-nie Doon, To see_the rose_ and
fresh_ and fair? How can ye chant,_ ye lit - tle birds,_And I ___ sae wea - ry,
wood-bine twine, And il - ka bird_sang o'__ its love,_And fond - ly sae_ did
fu'_ o' care? Thou'lt break my heart, thou warb - ling bird,_That wan - tons through the
I __ o' mine. Wi' light-some heart_I pu'd a rose,_Fu' sweet_ up - on__ its
flow-'ring thorn, Thou minds me o'_ de - part-ed joys,_De - part-ed nev - er to__ re-turn.
thorn - y tree, And my false lov - er stole_my rose,_But, ah!_ he left_the thorn wi' me.
D.C.

80. THE WRAGGLE TAGGLE GIPSIES

English folk-song

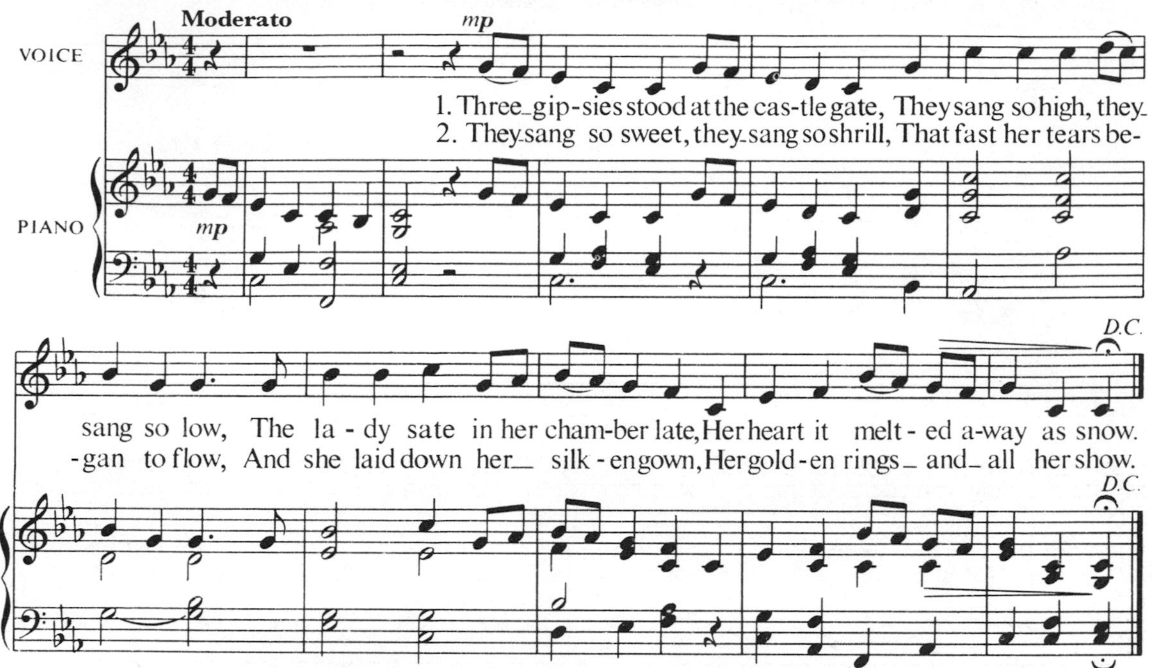
Moderato
mp
VOICE
PIANO
mp
1. Three gip-sies stood at the cas-tle gate, They sang so high, they sang so low, The la-dy sate in her cham-ber late, Her heart it melt-ed a-way as snow.
2. They sang so sweet, they sang so shrill, That fast her tears be-gan to flow, And she laid down her silk-en gown, Her gold-en rings and all her show.
D.C.
D.C.

3 She pluck-ed off her high-heeled shoes,
A-made of Spanish leather, O.
She would in the street, with her bare, bare feet,
All out in the wind and weather, O.

4 "O saddle to me my milk-white steed,
And go and fetch me my pony, O.
That I may ride and seek my bride,
Who is gone with the wraggle taggle gipsies, O."

5 O he rode high, and he rode low,
He rode through wood and copses too,
Until he came to an open field,
And there he espied his a-lady, O.

6 "What makes you leave your house and land,
Your golden treasures for to go?
What makes you leave your new-wedded lord,
To follow the wraggle taggle gipsies, O?"

7 "What care I for my house and land?
What care I for my treasure, O?
What care I for my new-wedded lord?
I'm off with the wraggle taggle gipsies, O!"

8 "Last night you slept on a goose-feather bed,
With the sheet turned down so bravely, O.
Tonight you'll sleep in a cold open field,
Along with the wraggle taggle gipsies, O."

9 "What care I for a goose-feather bed,
With the sheet turned down so bravely, O?
Tonight I'll sleep in a cold open field,
Along with the wraggle taggle gipsies, O."

81. WILL YE NO COME BACK AGAIN?

Scottish traditional tune, with words by Lady Nairne

Moderato
VOICE
PIANO
1. Bon - nie Char-lie's noo a - wa,
2. Ye trust - ed in your Hie- land men, They
Safe - ly o'er the friend-ly main, Mony a heart will break in twa,
trust - ed you, dear Char - lie; They kent your hid - ing in the glen,
Should he ne'er come back a-gain.
Death and ex - ile brav - ing.
Will ye no come back a-gain? Will ye no come
back a-gain? Bet-ter loved ye can-na be, Will ye no come back a-gain?
D.C.

3 Sweet's the laverock's note and lang,
Lilting wildly up the glen;
But aye to me he sings ae sang,
"Will ye no come back again?"
Will ye no etc.

82. WE BE THREE POOR MARINERS

English sea song, with tune and words from Ravenscroft's *Deuteromelia*, 1609

Moderato
mp
VOICE
PIANO
1. We be three poor mar - i-ners, Just new-ly from the seas; We spend our lives in jeo - par-dy, While oth-ers live at ease.
2. Care we not for mar - tial men Who do our states dis-dain; But we care for the mer - chant-men Who do our states main-tain.
mf
Come, let us dance the round, a-round, a-round; Come, let us dance the round, a-round, a-round,
To them we dance this round, a-round, a-round, To them we dance this round, a-round, a-round,
And he that is a bul - ly boy, Come pledge me on this ground, a-ground, a-ground.
D.C.

83. WALTZING MATILDA

Australian song, melody by Marie Cowan, words by A. B. Paterson

Moderato
VOICE
PIANO
mf
mf
1. Once a jol-ly swag-man camped by a bil-la-bong, Un-der the shade of a cool-i-bah tree, And he sang as he watched and wait-ed till his bil-ly boiled,
2. Down_came a jum-buck to drink_ at the bil-la-bong, Up jumped the swag-man and grabbed him with glee, And he sang as he stowed that jum-buck in his tuc-ker bag,
"You'll come a-waltz-ing Ma-til-da with me!
Waltz-ing Ma-til-da, waltz-ing Ma-til-da,

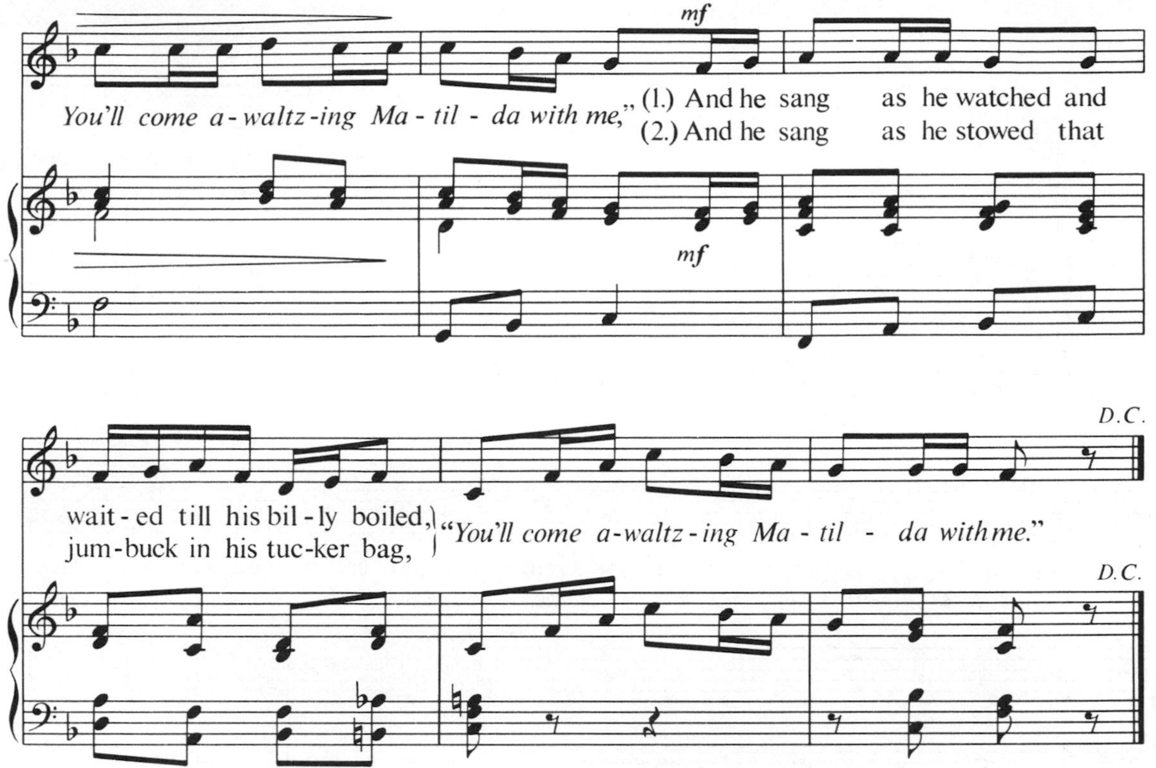
mf
You'll come a-waltz-ing Ma - til - da with me," (1.) And he sang as he watched and
(2.) And he sang as he stowed that
mf
D.C.
wait - ed till his bil - ly boiled,
jum-buck in his tuc-ker bag,
"You'll come a-waltz-ing Ma - til - da with me."
D.C.

3 Up rode the squatter, mounted on his thoroughbred,
Up rode the troopers, one, two, three:
"Whose that jolly jumbuck you've got in your tuckerbag?
You'll come a-waltzing Matilda with me.
Waltzing Matilda, waltzing Matilda,
You'll come a-waltzing Matilda with me.
Whose that jolly jumbuck you've got in your tuckerbag?
You'll come a-waltzing Matilda with me!"

4 Up jumped the swagman and sprang into the billabong,
"You'll never take me alive," said he.
And his ghost may be heard as you pass by that billabong:
"*You'll come a-waltzing Matilda with me.*
Waltzing Matilda, waltzing Matilda,
You'll come a-waltzing Matilda with me,"
And his ghost may be heard as you pass by that billabong:
"*You'll come a-waltzing Matilda with me."*

swagman: a man on tramp carrying his swag, a bundle wrapped up in a blanket
billabong: a waterhole in the dried-up bed of a river
jumbuck: a sheep
squatter: a sheep-farmer on a large scale

84. THE VICAR OF BRAY

English 17th-century tune, with 18th-century words

Moderato
VOICE
PIANO
mp
mp
1. In good King_Charles's gold - en days, When
2. When roy - al_James poss-essed the crown, And
loy - al - ty no harm meant, A zeal - ous_high church-man was I, And
Pop-ery came in fash - ion, The pe - nal_laws I hoot - ed down, And
so I got pre - fer - ment. To teach my_flock I ne - ver_missed, Kings
read the Dec - lar - a - tion. The Church of_Rome I found would_fit Full
were by_God ap - point - ed, And lost are_those that dare re - sist, Or
well my_con - sti - tu - tion, And I had_been a Jes - u - it But

mf
touch the Lord's an - oint - ed.
for the Rev - o - lu - tion.
And this is — law I
will main-tain Un - til my— dy - ing— day, Sir, That
what - so - ev - er king shall reign, I'll still be the Vi-car of Bray, Sir.
D.C.
mf
D.C.

3 When William was our King declared
To ease the nation's grievance,
With this new wind about I steered
And swore to him allegiance.
Old principles I did revoke,
Set conscience at a distance;
Passive obedience was a joke,
A jest was non-resistance.
And this is law etc.

4 When royal Anne became our Queen,
The Church of England's glory,
Another face of things was seen
And I became a Tory;
Occasional conformists base,
I blamed their moderation
And thought the Church in danger was
By such prevarication.
And this is law etc.

5 Th' illustrious house of Hanover
And Protestant succession,
To them I do allegiance swear—
While they can hold possession;
For in my faith and loyalty
I never more will falter,
And George my lawful King shall be—
Until the times do alter.
And this is law etc.

85. SONG OF THE WESTERN MEN

Cornish traditional tune, with words by the Rev. R.S. Hawker. Trelawny, Bishop of Bristol, was one of the seven bishops imprisoned in the Tower of London by King James II.

Boldly
VOICE
PIANO
mf
mf
1. A good sword and a trust - y hand! A mer - ry heart and true! King James - s's men shall un - der - stand What Corn - ish lads can do. And have they fixed the where and when? And
2. Out - spake their cap - tain brave and bold, A mer - ry wight was he: "If Lon - don Tower were Mich - ael's hold, We'll set Tre - law - ny free! We'll cross the Ta - mar, land to land, The
3. "And when we come to Lon - don Wall, A pleas - ant sight to view, Come forth, come forth, ye cow - ards all, Here's men as good as you! Tre - law - ny, he's in keep and hold, Tre -

shall Tre - law - ny die? Here's twen - ty thou - sand
Sev - ern is no stay, With 'One and all,' and
-law - ny, he may die, But twen - ty thou - sand
Corn - ish men Shall know the rea - son why!
hand in hand, And who shall bid us nay?"
Corn - ish bold Will know the rea - son why!"
f
A
f
good sword and a trus - ty hand! A mer - ry heart and true! King
James - s's men shall un - der-stand What Corn-ish lads can do.
D.C.
D.C.

86. THE OAK AND THE ASH

English traditional song (tune c. 1650)

Gently
VOICE
PIANO
p
1. A north-coun-try maid up to
2."While sad - ly I roam I re-
3."No doubt, did I please, I could
Lon-don had strayed, Al - though with her na - ture it did not a-gree; She_
-gret my dear home, Where_lads and young lass-es are mak-ing the hay; The_
mar - ry with ease; Where_maid - ens are fair ma-ny lov - ers will come; But_
wept and she sighed, and_bit-ter-ly she cried,"I_wish once a-gain in the north I could be.
bells they do ring, and the birds they do sing, The fields and the gar-dens are plea-sant and gay.
he whom I wed must be north-coun-try bred, And car-ry me back to my north-coun-try home.
Oh! the
mf
dim.
D.C.
oak, and the ash, and the bon-ny i-vy tree, They_flour-ish at home in my own coun-try."

87. MY BONNY CUCKOO

British folk-song

Moderato
VOICE
PIANO
p
1. My bon - ny cuc - koo,_ I tell thee true That through_the groves I'll_ rove with you: I'll rove with you un- -til the next spring And then my cuc-koo shall_sweet - ly sing. "Cuc-koo, Cuc-koo," un- -til the next spring, And then my cuc- koo shall_sweet - ly sing.
2. The ash and the haz-el shall sad - ly say, "My bon - ny cuc-koo, don't_go a - way, Don't go a - way, but tar - ry here And make_ the sea - son_ last all the year. Cuc-koo, Cuc-koo, pray tar - ry here, And sing_ for us through - out the year."
cresc.
dim.
D. S.
Ped.

88. THE MINSTREL BOY

Irish traditional tune, with words by Thomas Moore

Moderato
VOICE
PIANO
mp
1. The min - strel boy_ to the
2. The min - strel fell,_ but the
war is gone, In the ranks of death_you'll find him; His fa - ther's sword he has
foe-man's chain Could not bring his proud_ soul un - der; The harp he loved nev - er
gird - ed on, And his wild harp slung_ be - hind him.
spoke a - gain, For he tore its chords_ a - sun - der, And
mf
"Land of song!" said the war-rior-bard, "Though all the world be - trays_ thee, One
said, "No chains shall_ sul - ly thee, Thou soul of love and brav - er-y! Thy
sword, at least,_ thy_ rights shall guard, One_ faith-ful harp_ shall praise thee."
songs were made for the pure and free, They shall nev - er sound_ in slav - 'ry."
D.S.

89. THE MILLER OF DEE

English 17th-century tune, with 18th-century words

Steadily
VOICE
PIANO
mp
1. There was a jol - ly mil - ler once Lived
2. "I live by my mill, she is to me Like
3. Then like the mill - er, bold and free, Let
on the riv - er Dee, He worked and sang from morn till night, No
par - ent, child, and wife, I would not change my sta - tion For
us re - joice and sing, The days of youth were made for glee, And
mf
lark more blithe than he. And this the bur - den of his song For ev - er used to
a - ny oth-er in life. No law - yer, sur - geon, or doc - tor E'er had a groat from
time is on the wing. The song shall pass from me to thee, And round this jo - vial
be, "I care for no - bo - dy, no, not I, If no - bo - dy cares for me.
me, I care for no - bo - dy, no, not I, If no - bo - dy cares for me."
ring, And all in heart and voice, a - gree To sing, "Long live the King."
D.C.

90. THE MERMAID

English traditional song

Moderato
VOICE
PIANO
mf
1. One — Fri - day morn when
2. And — then up spoke the
we — set — sail, And our ship not far from — land, We —
cap-tain of our ship, Who at once our per - il did see, "I have
there did es - py — a — pret - ty, pret-ty maid, With a comb and a glass — in her
mar - ried a wife — in — fair — Lon-don town, And to-night she a wi - dow will
hand, her hand, her hand, With a comb and a glass — in her hand.
be, will be, will be, And to-night she a wi - dow will be."
f
While the

ra - ging seas_ did_ roar, And the stor - my winds did_ blow, And_
we jol - ly sai - lor boys were up, were up a - loft, And the land - lub - bers ly - ing down be-
- low, be - low, be - low, And the land - lub - bers ly - ing down be - low.
D.C.
D.C.

3 And then up spoke the little cabin boy,
And a fair-haired boy was he,
"I've a father and mother in fair Portsmouth town,
And tonight they will weep for me, for me, for me,
And tonight they will weep for me."

4 Then three times round went our gallant ship,
And three times round went she,
Then three times round went our gallant, gallant ship
And she sank to the bottom of the sea, the sea, the sea,
And she sank to the bottom of the sea.

91. MEN OF HARLECH

Welsh traditional song, with words by Thomas Oliphant. The song refers to the siege of Harlech Castle (held by Dafydd ap Jevan) by the Earl of Pembroke in the reign of Edward IV.

In march time
VOICE
PIANO
f
f
1. Hark! I hear the foe ad - vanc - ing, Barb - èd steeds are proud - ly pranc - ing,
Men of Har - lech, lie ye dream - ing? See ye not their fal - chions gleam - ing?
Hel - mets, in the sun-beams glanc - ing, Glit - ter through the trees.
While their pen - nants gai - ly stream - ing Flut - ter in the breeze.
From the rocks re - bound - ing, Let the war - cry sound - ing

Sum - mon all At Cam - bria's call, The haugh-ty_ foe_ sur - round-ing.
cresc.
Men of Har - lech, on to glo - ry! See, your_ ban - ner famed in sto - ry
cresc.
ff
Waves these burn - ing words be - fore ye, "Brit-ain scorns to yield."
ff
D.C.
D.C.

2 Mid the fray, see dead and dying,
Friend and foe together lying,
All around the arrows flying
Scatter sudden death.
Frightened steeds are wildly neighing
Brazen trumpets hoarsely braying,
Wounded men for mercy praying
With their parting breath.
See they're in disorder!
Comrades, keep close order!
Ever they
Shall rue the day
They ventured o'er the border.
Now the Saxon flees before us,
Vict'ry's banner floateth o'er us,
Raise the loud exulting chorus,
"Britain wins the field."

92. THE MALLOW FLING

British 18th-century tune, with words by A.H. Body

Not too fast
VOICE
PIANO
mp
1. Now the sun is shin-ing bright-ly,
2. Till the fires of night are burn-ing,
Old and young and stiff and spright-ly, Tread-ing swift-ly, tread-ing light-ly,
Dance they all, sad sor-row spurn-ing, Hap-py then to home re-turn-ing
Dance the Fling at Mal-low.
From the Fling at Mal-low.
mf
Oh, the danc-ing through the town, Oh, the pranc-ing
up and down, Priest and par-son, king and clown, Dance the Fling at Mal-low.
D.C.

93. LOCH LOMOND

Scottish traditional song (words and melody attributed to Lady John Scott)

Moderato
VOICE
PIANO
p
1. By yon bon-nie banks, and by yon bon-nie braes Where the sun shines bright on Loch Lo - mond, Where me and my true love were ev - er wont to gae, On the bon-nie, bon-nie banks o' Loch Lo - mond.
2. 'Twas there that we part - ed in yon sha - dy glen On the steep, steep side o' Ben Lo - mond, Where in pur-ple hue ma-ny Hie-land hills we'd view, And the moon com-ing out in the gloam - ing.
mf
Oh, ye'll tak' the high road and I'll tak' the low road, And I'll be in Scot-land a - fore ye; But me and my true love we'll nev-er meet a-gain On the bon-nie, bon-nie banks o' Loch Lo - mond.
D.C.

94. HIGH GERMANY

Somerset folk-song

In march time
VOICE
PIANO
mp
mp
1. O Pol - ly, love, O Pol - ly, the
2. O Har - ry, dear, O Har - ry, you
3. Oh, curs - ed were the cru - el wars that
rout has now be - gun, And_ we must march_ a - way at the
mind what I do say, My_ feet they are_ so_ ten - der, I
ev - er they should rise, And_ out of mer - ry_ Eng - land press
beat - ing of_ the drum: Go_dress your - self_ in_ all your best and come a - long with
can - not march_a - way, Be - sides, my dear - est_ Har - ry, though I'm in love with
many a lad_ like - wise! They pressed my Har - ry_ from_ me, like - wise my bro - thers
me, I'll take you to the cru - el wars in High_Ger - man - y.
thee, How am I fit for cru - el wars in High_Ger - man - y?
three, And sent them to the cru - el wars in High_Ger - man - y.
D.C.
D.C.

95. HEART OF OAK

Tune by William Boyce, with words by David Garrick.
The 'wonderful year' was 1759, the 'year of victories'.

Steadily
VOICE
PIANO
mf
1. Come, cheer up, my lads, 'tis to glo - ry we steer, To add some-thing more to this won - der - ful year; To hon-our we call you, not press you like slaves, For who are so free as the sons of the waves?
2. We ne'er see our foes but we wish them to stay, They ne - ver see us but they wish us a - way, If they run, why, we fol-low, and run them a - shore, For if they won't fight us, we can-not do more.
f
Heart of oak are our ships, Jol - ly tars are our men; We al - ways are rea - dy. Stea-dy, boys, stea-dy, We'll fight and we'll con - quer a - gain and a-gain.
D.C.

96. THE FLIGHT OF THE EARLS

Irish traditional tune, with words by A. P. Graves

Moderato
mp
VOICE
PIANO
mp
1. To o - ther shores a - cross the sea We
2. As slow - ly in - to_ dist - ance dim Your
3. Shall migh - ty * Es - pan's_ mar - tial praise Our
speed with swell-ing_ sail; Yet still there lin - gers_ on our lee A
sha - dow sinks_and_ dies, So o'er the o - cean's_ ut - most rim An -
pa - triot pul - ses_ still, And o'er your mem-'ry's_ fer - vent rays For
phan-tom In - nis - fail. Oh, fear not, fear not, gen - tle ghost, Your sons shall turn un-
-oth-er realm_shall_rise. New hills shall swell, new vales ex-pand, New ri - vers wind-ing
ev-er cast_a_chill? Oh no! we live for your re - lief, Till, home from a - lien
mp
-true! Tho' fain to fly_ your_ love - ly coast, They leave their hearts_with_ you.
flow, But could we for_ a_ fos - ter land Your mo - ther love_fore - go?
earth, We share the smile_that_gilds your grief, The tear that gems_your_mirth.
D. C.
mp
D. C.

* Espan's = Spain's

97. DRINK TO ME ONLY

Tune by an unknown composer, c. 1770, to words by Ben Jonson

With movement
VOICE
PIANO
p
1. Drink to me on - ly with thine eyes, And
2. I sent thee late a ro - sy wreath, Not
I will pledge with mine,
so much hon'-ring thee
mp
Or leave a kiss with - in the cup And I'll not ask for
As giv-ing it a hope that there It could not with-ered
mf
wine; The thirst that from the soul doth rise Doth ask a drink di-
be; But thou there-on didst on - ly breathe, And sendst it back to
-vine, But might I of Jove's nec - tar sup I would not change for thine.
me, Since when it grows, and smells, I swear, Not of it-self, but thee.
D.C.

98. DARBY KELLY

Tune by John Whitaker, with words adapted from Charles Dibdin

Briskly
VOICE
PIANO
mf
1. My grand - sire beat the drum com-plete, His
2. A son he had, who was my dad, The
3. And now, small blame, I bear the name And

name was Dar - by Kel - ly O! No lad so true_ at rat - tat-too, At
sec - ond Dar - by Kel - ly O! As quick and true_ at rat - tat-too, At
drum of Dar - by Kel - ly O! My - self as true_ to rat - tat-too, To

roll - call or re - veil - lez O! When Marl-bro's name first rose to fame, So
roll - call or re - veil - lez O! When great Wolfe died, his count - ry's pride, To
roll - call or re - veil - lez O! With Wel - ling - ton, old Ire - land's son, I've

mf
proud he roll'd the Point of War, At Blen - heim he and
arms, to arms the fath - er beat, Each dale and hill re -
beat the Moun-seers out of Spain, And now we march through
mf
Ra - mil - lies Fired all our cham - pions to the core, And Oh, his wrist had
-mem - bers still How loud and long, how clear and sweet! And when for home from
lau - rel arch And wav - ing ban - ners home a - gain; And as my sticks the
mf
such a twist, When home they march'd with row - dow - dow, With
off the foam He led the march with row - dow - dow, Och!
same old tricks They play with patt - 'ring row - dow - dow, Man,
mf
D.C.
one great shout the boys came out, The girls they gazed, you don't know how!
what a shout the lads let out, The las - ses looked, you don't know how!
wo - man, child, they've all gone wild, The girls they gaze, you don't know how!
D.C.

99. BONNIE DUNDEE

Scottish traditional tune, with words by Sir Walter Scott

Moderato
mf
VOICE
PIANO
1. To the Lords of Con-ven-tion 'twas Clav'r-house who spoke: "Ere the King's crown shall fall there are crowns to be broke, Then each cav-a - lier who loves hon-our and me, Let him fol-low the bon-net of Bon-nie Dun-dee."
2. Dun- dee he is moun-ted, he rides up the street, The bells are rung back-ward, the drums they are beat, But the Pro - vost, douce man, said, "Just e'en let him be, The gude town is weel quit o' that De'il o' Dun-dee."
f
Come fill up my cup, come fill up my can, Come

sad-dle your hor-ses, and call out your men, Come op-en the West Port, and
let me gang free, And it's room for the bon-nets of Bon-nie Dun-dee.
ff
D.C.

3 There are hills beyond Pentland, and lands beyond Forth,
Be there lords in the Lowlands, they've chiefs in the North;
There are wild Du-nie-was-sals, three thousand times three,
Will cry "Hoi" for the bonnet of Bonnie Dundee.
Come fill up my cup etc.

4 "Then away to the hills, to the caves, to the rocks—
Ere I own a usurper, I'll crouch with the fox;
And tremble, false Whigs, in the midst of your glee,
You have not seen the last of my bonnet and me."
Come fill up my cup etc.

100. THE BAY OF BISCAY

Tune by John Davy, with words by Andrew Cherry

Steadily
mf
VOICE
PIANO
mf
1. Loud roars the dread - ful
2. Now dashed up - on the
thun - der, The rain a de - luge show'rs, The
bil - low, Our op - 'ning tim - bers creak, Each
clouds were rent a - sun - der By light - ning's vi - vid
fears a wa - t'ry pil - low, None stops the dread - ful
pow'rs; The night was drear and dark, Our
leak. To cling to slip - p'ry shrouds Each

poor de - vo - ted bark Till next day, there she
breath - less sea - man crowds, As she lay, till the

D.C.
1
2
lay, In the Bay of Bis - cay, O! O!
day, In the Bay of Bis cay, O! O!
1
2
D.C.

3 At length the wished-for morrow
  Breaks through the hazy sky,
Absorbed in silent sorrow
  Each heaved a bitter sigh.
The dismal wreck to view
Struck horror to the crew,
As she lay, on that day,
In the Bay of Biscay, O!

4 Her yielding timbers sever,
  Her pitchy seams are rent,
When Heav'n, all-bounteous ever,
  Its boundless mercy sent.
A sail in sight appears,
We hail her with three cheers.
Now we sail, with the gale,
From the Bay of Biscay, O!

Printed by
Halstan & Co. Ltd., Amersham, Bucks., England